Advance Praise for
Leaving Revolution: How We Are Learning to Let Go and Move On

"*Leaving Revolution* has forever changed how I think about leaving. Dr. Wisdom deftly weaves theory, her personal experience, and more than 100 interviews to help us reconsider the role of letting go and moving on in our lives. Whether you're a leaver or a stayer, you must read this book."
> – **Ramani Durvasula, Author of** *Should I Stay or Should I Go?* **and Professor of Psychology, California State University Los Angeles**

"In my mid-20s, I left a bad marriage and a career I hated to start a new life in a distant city. Dr. Wisdom clearly articulates what I couldn't express then: leaving 'is about coming into our own power.' Her book will help you make sense of why you leave – or stay – and what this means for your own life story."
> – **David Hochfelder, Associate Professor of History, University at Albany, SUNY**

"Thinking about leaving? Then you need to read this book. Part memoir, part how-to guide, *Leaving Revolution* perfectly captures the post-pandemic moment of resignations, breakups, divorces, and more to help us forever think differently about leaving and staying."
> – **Michele Gregoire Gill, Professor of Educational Psychology, University of Central Florida**

"One of life's frequently asked questions is 'Should I stay or should I go?' I used to flip a coin, but there's so much more to consider: logistics, rational and emotional obstacles, adventure vs. commitment. Our identities are largely shaped by leave/stay decisions. Dr. Wisdom takes her personal experiences and reflections with those of more than a hundred others, and fits them into a historical, literary, and cultural context. Yes, human restlessness, finding ourselves, and finding where we want to be is ancient and universal. We are now (as we have been before) in a time of great upheaval and uncertainty. *Leaving Revolution*'s solid research and lived experience is garnished with humor, hope, and kindness. Any of the stories could be yours. You are not alone, and your path awaits."

    – **Gerry Vogel, Librarian, Avon Lake, Ohio**

"*Leaving Revolution* addresses the complex decisions we all make as we choose to move on. As a home-leaver, job-leaver, and relationship-stayer, I am proud I raised a daughter who wrote such a powerful book about leaving. Reading this book has helped me understand her, understand leaving, and understand myself."

    – **Georgette King, Author's Mom**

"'We just change.' This line sums up life so perfectly. *Leaving Revolution* book is an amazing resource for anyone facing change in their life who is looking for guidance and direction on how to make the big decision. It will not only allow you to see yourself in its pages and to find your how-to-guide of choosing to stay or go, but it will give you an understanding of the people around you and possibly bring healing to areas where you may not have had closure."

    – **Dawn Taylor, Trauma Specialist and Coach, The Taylor Way**

"With a compelling history of confronting life's challenges and pursuing her best self, Jennifer Wisdom frames the art of letting go with personal stories, vulnerability, and logic. This book provides me with a new mindset and overdue validation for some of the scariest decisions of my life. I wish I knew then what I know now."

    – **Shannon Golden, Self-Employed Research Consultant, and 2021 member of The Great Resignation**

LEAVING
REVOLUTION

How We Are Learning
to Let Go and Move On

WINDING PATHWAY BOOKS

Jennifer Wisdom, PhD

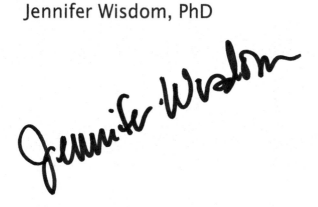

Published by Winding Pathway Books

WINDING PATHWAY BOOKS

ISBN (paperback): 978-1-954374-42-3
ISBN (ebook): 978-1-954374-43-0
ISBN (hardcover): 978-1-954374-41-6

Editors: Fiona Marshall and Martha Bullen
Book design: Katie Dooley at PaperLime
Photo credit: Diego G. Diaz

For more information or bulk orders, visit: www.leadwithwisdom.com

Printed in the United States of America

CONTENTS

INTRODUCTION

I was raised on fantastic and powerful stories of leaving. My mother's father, born in the 1890s in Syria, was hidden by his parents for nearly a year when he was a child because young males were being conscripted to fight in an ongoing war. When he was around 13, a cousin with a visa died, and my grandfather assumed his identity, traveling through Turkey and France to emigrate to the U.S. My mother's maternal grandparents left the poverty of Naples, Italy in the early 1900s to make a better life in the U.S. My father's ancestors left Holland for the new world in 1663, landing in what is now Brooklyn. These stories fascinated me as a child. Radically changing one's life by uprooting in this way, and seizing the opportunity to move across the world, seemed extraordinarily exciting.

As it happened, my early childhood provided opportunities to experience both the good and not-so-good aspects of leaving. After my parents' divorce when I was three, my mother, brother, and I (and later my stepfather) moved several times. Moves from economic necessity became an unsatisfying exercise in seeking bigger, better homes in fancier neighborhoods. These later childhood moves were very disruptive to me, resulting in the loss of recently earned friends and known neighborhoods, and leaving me with little sense of roots. On the other hand, I became a young expert in the logistics of moving, packing, and unpacking, saying goodbye, and making new friends. By 18, I had lived in nine homes and had only two good friends who had known me for more than three years. I felt in my bones, though, that my adventure was just starting. And I was right.

Almost everyone in the world has an experience of leaving. They leave one home for another as a child, as I did. They leave home for work or college or marriage. They leave relationships, jobs, religions, and communities. People also leave for adventures, for freedom, solitude, to take a break, or because they don't know why but they just have to get out of Here. Leaving is the stuff of history (the *Declaration of Independence*), great literature (*The Odyssey*), movies' most dramatic moments (like the famous last scene in *Casablanca*) and television's tearjerkers (when the soldiers of *M*A*S*H*'s 4077th finally left Korea for home). Many of us have struggled with whether to leave, and ultimately decided to stay. Leaving can also provide us with our first experience of grief. Some of us choose leaving, others have it thrust upon us, and have been left behind when others have left us.

As I was contemplating another opportunity to leave, I looked for a book that could help me think through the process of leaving and its role in my life. Maybe I hoped to find answers to my past and its many upheavals, or maybe I wanted to know more about the psychological journey of moving on. As a psychologist, I study the mind and behavior, and I'm particularly fascinated by how individuals interact with and excel in their environments. I have studied workplaces for years; I've heard from hundreds, if not thousands, of employees on why they love or hate their workplaces. I have also worked as a therapist, with a front row seat to family dysfunction and dissolution. I am scientifically interested in the mechanisms and stages involved in leaving, while as a person, leaving seems to be written into my DNA. Not finding such a book, I decided to write it.

As I was writing, I discovered that I am far from alone in leaving. Americans are leaving jobs, leaving partners, dropping out of school, and completely leaving the plans they had for their lives. Especially since the pandemic upended many norms, Americans are refusing to fall in line working at the same job, staying in the same place, and doing the same thing they've always done. They're looking for even more out of life. In looking to understand my own patterns of leaving, I stumbled upon a leaving revolution.

I have three goals for this book:
- I want readers to understand that leaving is an integral part of living. I'm a firm proponent of persisting through

difficulty. That said, letting go of what is no longer working can be a significant strength and a big step toward fulfillment. Leaving can sometimes be the healthiest thing we can do.

- I would like readers to be more courageous in choosing to leave. I provide a set of steps gleaned from interviews with more than 100 leavers and stayers to help think through whether leaving is the right choice, and if it is, how to make it happen.

- I hope that this book can help those who have left better to integrate their experiences, deal with leaving-associated grief, and accept themselves and their decisions. Even when our new life is richer and more satisfying than what we left behind, it can take time to make sense of it all. I hope this book can also help all of us feel more compassionate about our leaving experiences, and when others choose to leave.

This book has three primary sections, informed by my interviews with more than a hundred amazing people, by my own experiences of leaving and staying, and by my background as a clinical psychologist and researcher. In Part 1, I look at why and how we leave. Chapter 1: Leaving, describes some of the approaches to leaving experts have identified, such as psychological theory about leaving home, organizational theory about leaving jobs, and even shamanic approaches of leaving as part of the essential journey of the archetypal Hero. I then (in Chapter 2: Who, and What We Leave,) describe who and what we leave, from jobs to partners, homes, religions, and identities. Next (in Chapter 3) I briefly outline the six steps many of us, but not all, go through when we have the luxury to decide whether to leave.

Part 2 goes into depth about each of these steps. I hope to dispel the notion that leaving equals failure because it absolutely does not. There are many, many reasons for leaving, often to help us grow and find joy. Chapters 4-9 analyze the six steps of awareness, confidence, decision, preparation, the actual leaving itself, and the integration of our experience.

Part 3 discusses situations when leaving is not your choice, and whether you can ever go back after you've left. Chapters 10-12 look at what happens if you're fired from a job or left by a partner, how and why people may revisit the past, and what to do if you can't leave.

As you read on, I encourage you to think about my good friend Dr. Kristina Hallett's macaroni and cheese theory of personal growth. Really – her mac and cheese theory provides a lot of insight on leaving! Her theory is this: When we are six years old, we love boxed macaroni and cheese. We loved that near-neon orange color, the small elbow pasta, the cheesy soup that drenched the pasta. Boxed mac and cheese was our six-year-old self's idea of fine dining. Eventually, as we got older, many of us found that we are not as big a fan of it. We perhaps developed more sophisticated palates that prefer sirloin, or lobster, or moussaka. We may rarely eat mac and cheese anymore. So what happened? We just changed. Our tastes changed. Note the macaroni and cheese did not change at all. There is nothing wrong with it. It's not bad. We don't need to feel bad about no longer liking it. We don't have to feel guilty about leaving it. In fact, sometimes we may reminisce about mac and cheese and have some. It's okay.

Many times, we need to leave for various reasons – the situation no longer is a good fit for us, we have outgrown it, we are no longer learning from it, we decide we just don't like it anymore, or thousands of other reasons. If we think we need to move on from a job, relationship, home, or anything else, this book can help us think through the process and decide if we really need to leave. And if we do decide to go, it doesn't mean the person or job or place we're leaving is bad now, or that it was bad before, or that it was a mistake to ever get involved. Sometimes we just need to move on. It's okay.

I wrote this book in my office, in the back of a cab, in a library, on an airplane, in a hotel room, and on the subway. I wrote it when my work and adventures took me to Bangladesh, Dubai, Johannesburg, London, Nairobi, Brazil, and Los Angeles. I interviewed people in all of these places and in other places as well, including on many plane, train, and subway trips. The people I interviewed were fascinating and generous and kind, and their leaving stories are incredibly brave. When I told people I was writing about leaving and asked if they had a leaving story, absolute strangers told me about getting divorced from abusive spouses, about knowing something wasn't right in their family and struggling to fix it, of being left and having to pick up the pieces, of leaving a job that was no longer a good fit, of wanting to leave but feeling obligated to stay.

My questions opened conversations and stories in a way that talking about the weather just can't. Many people told me that they appreciated the opportunity to talk about leaving, and that they now think of it differently. Some individuals shut down the conversation initially, then came back and said, "I've been thinking about your question..." People I interviewed sometimes shed tears when they remembered the challenges they had struggled with, and sometimes they beamed proudly while sharing how far they had come. Nearly everyone told me they hoped their stories and struggles would help others. I am so grateful to everyone who shared their stories with me, and I am so honored to share them in turn with you, the reader.

In many ways the theme of this book is about coming into your own power. Whether you choose to leave or to stay – or a little of both – this book discusses life skills to make the journey easier. How to think through your options, have difficult conversations with yourself and with others, decide what's best for you, and then make it happen – these topics are all explored in this book in the hope that they will empower you and serve you well. In my experience, it's also helpful to consider the perspectives of stayers as well as leavers, so that you can understand your default modes and use this increased understanding to determine what's best for you, instead of repeating any unconscious or compulsive behavior and letting it dominate your life.

It's important to let go of any part of the past that holds you back so you can embrace your future. It's vital to make your own way through life, to understand when things aren't working, and to make an active choice to change your circumstances and to improve your life. It is my hope that this book helps you identify key aspects of their own leaving experiences, whether they are considering leaving, are in the process of departing, or are reflecting on your past leaving experiences.

Each chapter includes both my own personal experience, and stories of the brave and kind people I interviewed about some of the most difficult decisions of their lives. There is practical advice about what to do, as well as emotional advice to help you move through your process. Regardless of where you may be in your leaving or staying process – just thinking about leaving, in the middle of it, or looking back – this book can help you be thoughtful, courageous, and true to yourself in making a path that will delight you. Welcome to the leaving revolution!

Part 1

Chapter 1: Leaving and Staying

Leaving is universal. Nearly all of us alive today are ancestors of people who made brave choices to leave their homes, families, and countries to seek better lives. From ancient people departing the birthplace of civilization in Africa to establish new communities in Europe and Asia, to 16th century explorers who sailed around the world in search of adventures and gold, most of us can trace our lineage back to people who left home to face the unknown. Every day, thousands of people make decisions to leave their job, their partner, their home, or other situations that are not working for them. Unfortunately, thousands more stay in miserable situations, and struggle with their inability to move on or take action to fulfill their destiny. It doesn't have to be this way.

History, literature, and the arts are full of the daring, the desperate, and the plain fed up, who leave their homes, their families, and their jobs in search of a better life. This book incorporates perspectives from history, psychological theory, literature and movies, interviews with more than 100 people, along with my own experience. Throughout this book, my aim is to help readers understand more about the universal experiences of leaving.

I am a professional leaver. My childhood was a barrage of moving: every two years or so, we changed homes and schools, with nine moves by the time I was 18. My parents were not in the military; they moved when my parents divorced, for a safer place to live, for financial reasons, when my mother remarried, for work, for a safer place not on a main road, and twice for "no good reason" according to my mother.

Decades later, they continued to move every few years in search of the home that will bring them happiness. As a kid, I started writing about leaving each time we moved: what I would miss, what I was looking forward to, how I felt about the move. These journal entries evolved as I grew older to catalogue break-ups, job changes, the actual moves (now at 27 times), and other major life decisions: the circumstances around the dilemma, what I thought my options were, and justification for making the decision I did. This habit would serve me well.

As I continued into adulthood, I was determined to not repeat my parents' patterns of leaving. And yet, I became a leaver anyway. I tried quite diligently to make things work, and somehow, I still ended up leaving. Relationship not working? After struggles to make it work, to give more than I needed to, to negotiate, to dig deep and to be patient, I still ended up leaving. Job not providing fulfillment, stimulation, or advancement? I tried so hard to make that work, too – finding aspects of it that I loved, changing how I interacted with difficult people, seeking similar positions in the same organization; and yet, eventually, I still left. Moving was always for a good reason: for a better school, for a more fulfilling job, for a bigger place. I became expert at recouping my losses, salvaging, and turning loss into gain – if nothing else, I turned these frequent moves into strength by remodeling houses before I moved on. Selling them for a profit made the experience at least financially positive.

Please don't think leaving has been easy for me. Leaving is never easy. I don't care any less about my coworkers or partners or career or homes than other people. I'm not flaky or flighty or unreliable. I'm not disloyal or disturbed. I never leave out of anger or in a huff. In fact, the whole process of moving on always feels agonizing to me. At the same time, in each of these past experiences, leaving was the exact thing I had to do. In each situation, I tried my best, but I can't *not* leave when things aren't working. My perspective, honed over many years and through many struggles, is that life is too short to be unhappy, and we are all responsible for our own growth and development.

I have occasionally longed to understand what it must be like for those who have lived in the same community (or even the same house!) all their lives. How it feels to have friendships that go back to childhood, or to celebrate a 25th wedding anniversary. That sort of long-term stability has not been my lot. I have a restlessness that makes me much more willing to leave situations than most people I know, while never quite reaching full nomad stage. I'm aware that many people might judge leavers as being "too flighty" or not having the persistence to stick out tough situations. And leavers might be thinking that stayers aren't ambitious enough. But there is no one right choice. We are all complex individuals with our own challenges and patterns of leaving and staying, as I shall discuss.

As I was researching the concept of leaving, I found that essential transitions run deep for almost all of us. Many of our defining critical moments – the ones that forever changed our destiny – are about leaving. As children, we practice and learn the delight and fear of leaving by playing games like peek-a-boo and hide-and-seek. History, literature, and the movies examine, glamorize, and traumatize leaving. The struggle over whether to leave is a nearly universal experience, regardless of whether the person ends up going or staying. And yet, I could find no resources that provided a comprehensive approach to understanding the concept of leaving or reference the leaving revolution we find ourselves in.

With all of that in mind, welcome to this book. I hope it will help you understand the concept of leaving better, to place its role in our lives in perspective and to view it more creatively. Leaving is often a wrenching or an upheaval. It can sometimes leave scars. But before every arrival there is a departure. Whenever we move on, we are leaving something behind and going somewhere else.

Why we stay
Part of what is so powerful about leaving is that it raises deep-seated fears to do with security and survival. These primal fears are often

what keep people in less than satisfactory situations – what makes us stay.

- *I'll be alone.* Whether we're leaving a partner or slinking out of the Garden of Eden, basic fears of abandonment can be overwhelming, sometimes dating from babyhood when being left was literally a death threat. In leaving our daily support system – be it a religion, a partner, a peer group, or neighbors, we may connect subconsciously with ancient terrors of being isolated and lonely, not just now but forever. This fear can be very real and often makes us rethink whether we really want to leave.

- *I'll go hungry.* Moving on can also evoke fears of not being able to meet our fundamental needs. Adam and Eve had to find a new home and life and to work for their food. If we choose to leave whatever comfort we experienced in the relationship, home, or job, we might not know how we'll earn money, or make dinner, or take care of ourselves. Even though we were utterly miserable before, an empty stomach (and its metaphorical equivalents) is a powerful fear and may motivate us to stay put.

- *I won't know who I am.* Adam and Eve were God's chosen children ... until they weren't. If we're no longer a husband or wife, no longer an employee, no longer who we thought we were (or who others thought we were), that can be a real jolt to our sense of self. We have carefully cultivated an identity around our romantic, family, colleague, friend, and neighborly relationships. If everyone in our lives knows us as part of married couple Jack and Sara, Daniel's mother, an employee of the health department, or as the woman who always speaks up at meetings, what will happen if we leave? How will people know us, and more importantly, how will we know ourselves? Choosing to leave our place in the world, our corner where we're nestled in all these relationships and daily habits, raises all kinds of fears about who we are, and who we will become.

- *This is as good as it gets.* We have a job, a partner, and a place to live – maybe this as good as it gets? It doesn't matter if our job is a grind, our relationship all but over, and our living situation untenable – maybe this is the best life has to offer? We may tell ourselves that if we stretch our luck too far and ask for more than what we have, it's bound to end in failure. We may worry about being arrogant or out of turn, as in the "Who do I think I am?" question. As in, "*Who am I* to reject this very generous Garden-of-Eden offer to have almost everything I need in exchange for knowledge?" or, "*Who am I* to reject a comfortable job that pays the bills?" or, "*Who am I* to leave an okay relationship in search for one that's more meaningful?" or, "*Who am I* to declare the status quo is no longer good enough for me?" These are tough questions, and they deserve thoughtful answers.
- *It's all my fault.* When we leave, we take responsibility. This means that whatever happens next is our fault. If we reach for better and, like Icarus, fly too close to the sun and fall to the ground, we will be greeted by a chorus of tsk-tsking and, "I told you so." We believe that we brought upon ourselves every lonely, hungry, and frightened moment that we experience after we leave, because we dared to be different, to change, and to leave what was known and safe.

It's completely understandable that these fears are enough to make many of us stay in the job, the marriage, the community, or the not-quite-me identity for years and years because the alternative seems so – terrifying! We may be miserable, but we're safe. These fears are real, and they run deep in what it means to be human. Our insecurities deserve to be acknowledged and respected. And yet … many of us do leave. We find the courage, the gumption, and the oomph to declare that we are not happy, that we deserve better, and that we are going to face our fears and go for it. Sometimes, we do this from one day to the next. Other times it can be helpful to do it slowly, and to start by making small changes towards the life we want.

Approaches to leaving

Given that leaving is a near-universal experience, it is not surprising that there are many approaches to understanding how and why we leave, and stories that underscore its role in our lives.

- *Hero's journey.* I'll start with my favorite approach to understanding leaving: through the journey of the archetypical Hero. The journey of the Hero is a very old concept. It can be seen in our most ancient stories, such as that of Odysseus in Homer's epic, *The Odyssey,* and of Beowulf in the eponymous Old English epic poem. It has been described by mythologist Joseph Campbell, [1] with updates from poet and activist Robert Bly. [2] The hero's journey informs the story lines of our favorite literary and screen heroes, such as the original *Star Wars* movies where Luke Skywalker is the hero, and even in the *Harry Potter* children's literature series. The hero can, of course, be a heroine, and the hero's myth has been consistently updated by feminist thinkers such as psychotherapist Maureen Murdock.[3] Please interpret the Hero's gender as suits you best; I use the feminine pronoun here.

  The Hero's story is, briefly: The Hero has earthly parents who provide structure and teach important lessons. The Hero also has magical parents who connect her to a mystical destiny. At some point, a special teacher instructs the Hero about the world, and the Hero gains a glimpse of a magical destiny that requires her to leave home. After making the difficult decision to go, the Hero finds that the big world is not as safe as it was at home. She is aided in discovering her true calling by a magical teacher and by other allies, who provide information and help the Hero overcome challenges. At some point, the Hero (or the person the Hero was before starting her adventures) dies and is reborn to fight the biggest fight there is, a fight in which she engages with all her personal demons. After victory, the Hero finds her way back into the world, forever a changed person, bringing gifts back to her community.

What I like so much about this story is that *leaving* is essential to the Hero's path. When the Hero turns away from her true calling, she becomes weaker and loses power (such as by becoming ill or having bad things happen) until she finally decides to face her destiny. (I also like this storyline because it offers the Hero a second chance, or even more chances if needed! One bad decision doesn't have to rule your life.) The Hero's Journey supports the commonly held belief that if we are to become our true selves, at some point all of us must step out of our comfort zone to do something new, to struggle with it, and to overcome the related obstacles. Of course, that doesn't mean we all have to physically leave our homes or jobs or families immediately in search of fulfillment. I interpret the Hero's journey as illustrating the need to stay alert for what is and is not working for us, and to be bold enough to make changes when necessary, so that we can achieve our destiny and live as our true selves.

- *Psychological approaches.* From infancy, we start learning to differentiate what is "me" and what is "not me." Ideally, as babies we develop a "secure base"[4] with our caregiver(s) from which we can then explore the world. While these explorations lead to mastery of our own agency in the world, they also create a sense of separation from the caregiver, which we then must manage autonomy vs. dependence. How we manage this separation is related to how we relate to other people in our lives.

Sometimes, however, leaving can become problematic, such as when a person leaves others to protect himself from anxiety and abandonment. Deep shame can lead someone to justify leaving to avoid feeling like a victim. Frequent leaving may also serve to help maintain an illusion of omnipotence, that is, to help someone feel in control and in power. "I will leave you first before you can leave me" can be a defense against helplessness. Paradoxically, we can get stuck in replaying our leaving scenarios repeatedly to re-enact the situation in which we had no control. For example, we may leave lovers and partners pre-emptively in a reenactment of the way a parent abandoned us in our early years, asserting power we didn't have in childhood. By choosing to leave on our terms instead of someone else's, we can create a corrective emotional experience of a leaving situation in which we have more control.

For those of us who grew up without a secure base, a close relationship with a sensitive therapist can create a therapeutic alliance, which can serve as a similar base from which to explore the world and forge new relationships. A therapeutic relationship can serve as a healthy and authentic caregiving situation in which a person's expectations, wishes, and beliefs can play out. The therapist's responsiveness and consistency can materially assist the person in reducing distress, resolving challenges, and increasing their capacity to solve future problems and no-win situations.

This said, leaving a therapeutic relationship can provide a healthy opportunity to recreate leaving experiences in our lives. Indeed, this can be a move towards real freedom. We can perceive endings as if they are death, a completion, independence, freedom, accomplishment, or a joyful moment of maturation and "leaving home." How we choose to interpret this is, of course, up to us.

- *Leaving as power.* Leaving is not the only way to demonstrate control and power. Staying can be equally powerful. The justice system, however, tends to view leaving an abusive employer or spouse as evidence confirming the other person's behavior was inappropriate, and staying as evidence that, "It wasn't that bad." This somewhat negates the possibility of staying as a form of powerful resistance. Although the U.S. was founded on leaving, in that many people left their countries of origin to live here, and although leaving is often a demonstration of our autonomy, it is often true that leaving only indirectly creates change. Staying put and using our voice to change the situation is an equally important option, and our voice is especially valuable when there are significant barriers to leaving (such as sexual harassment or physical abuse).

There is a fiction that employees and employers – and men and women – are always equally free to leave, when the truth is much more complicated. Women often have fewer financial resources and higher family obligations that make it more difficult for them to move away, leave a spouse, or quit a job. Legal expert Martha Mahoney[5] writes, "It is a peculiarity of the abuse of women that we are expected to 'leave' the very centers of our lives whether or not we have anywhere to go." It is worth pointing out that we all have the *right* to stay – especially when we risk heavy loss by moving on.

In this book, leaving is one of possible directions our lives can take. I highly respect those who choose to stay, either to hold onto gains made or to make change from within. This book is to promote the conscious and intentional thinking-through of options to help us reach our own highest good.

- *Behavioral science models.* As a psychologist and researcher, I am intrigued by behavioral science models that apply to leaving. There is a rich scientific literature of models about decision making in low-stakes or high-stakes situations. Here are a few of my favorite behavioral science theories.

- The *sunk cost fallacy*[6] says that we often don't leave something because we've invested time, effort, or money, even if it would be in our best interest to leave. For example, people often stay in relationships that aren't working because they've already been together (or "invested") several years. We continue to eat more than we want to because we've already paid for the food. When we consider sunk costs, though, we are factoring in influences in addition to the current alternatives. We are letting our guilt or regret about the initial investment cloud our decisions. I try to use the sunk cost fallacy to spur myself to act on the decision in front of me; however, there are also some provocative suggestions that considering costs already invested could be useful in the context of creating a coherent narrative about ourselves and our decision making.[7]

- The *investment model*[8] of leaving takes the sunk costs even further. The investment model has been applied to the concept of leaving abusive relationships. It states that people decide to leave abusive relationships because of: how satisfied they are (how much a partner fulfills basic needs), the quality of alternatives to the relationship (how desirable the best available alternative is), how much has been invested already (the magnitude and importance of resources attached to a relationship that would be lost or less valuable if the relationship ended; essentially the sunk costs), and commitment (intent to persist in the relationship and feelings of attachment). Although this model is maybe a bit dry for day-to-day application, the concepts it evokes are all discussed in this book. Chapter 6, Decision, for example, discusses how to think logically about options, even when we may decide based on intuition or emotion.

- *Loss aversion*[9] also factors into decisions about leaving. Loss aversion describes that the impact of losses feels much worse to us than the impact of gains feels good. We feel losses more acutely than gains, so of course we try harder to avoid losses, which can bias our decision-making.

- *Opportunity cost*[10] is the benefit that we would have received from an option we didn't choose. So, if we spend the afternoon binge watching a new show, the opportunity cost is that we did not exercise or work on our novel or spend time with our friends. We are not very good at estimating opportunity costs, because to do so requires evaluating the costs and benefits of each option available to us and weighing them against each other. We don't tend to do that in our day-to-day lives, but I discuss the strategy of writing down options and actively considering what we really want later in the book.

- Finally, our greatest hits of behavioral science related to leaving also includes our desire to maintain the *status quo*.[11] When it comes down to it, we often follow the idiom, "Better the devil you know than the devil you don't," which means we prefer to deal with what we are familiar with, even if it's not ideal, instead of risking the unknown. We do this even though making a change often makes us happier, and even if that change was precipitated by something as simple as a coin toss (See Levitt's fascinating article[12] on life decisions in the For Further Reading section).

What should we learn from these behavioral science theories? First, as humans, we are all subject to making decisions that are irrational, based on emotion, or otherwise not necessarily in our best interests. Second, despite all our flaws in thinking, many of us have satisfying and enjoyable lives, we learn to live with our decisions, and we get better over time. That's not nothing!

- *Shamanic approaches to leaving.*[13] How many times have we heard, "You didn't choose the family you were born into"? Shamans, people who work with spirit and energy, would say that we *did* choose our families. Many shamans believe in multiple lifetimes, after each of which we meet with a life administrator (I want that job!), with whom we discuss the life that just ended, what we learned, and what we have left to learn. We then work with this administrator to choose our next life circumstances, ones that that will provide the greatest opportunity for us to learn whatever we need to learn. Together we decide whether we should have wealthy or poor parents, a loving or a harsh environment, and any number of other circumstances to maximize our learning potential. Once we decide, then whoosh! We are born into our next life, and we (usually) forget the previous lives together with the all-important between-lives discussion.

When I first heard this model, I felt such relief. The "original sin" model of Christianity never did fit well with me. And spending my life working off someone else's sin (though I still think Eve was framed!) did not seem appealing, fair, or appropriate in any way. The idea that I chose my circumstances was liberating. When I was unhappy, I could ask myself, why would I choose this opportunity? What is it I thought I could learn from this? What do I need to learn from it now? Do I choose to stay in this situation? (If there's something more to learn), or to leave it? (If I determine there's not much more I can learn). That's such a helpful perspective compared to the old concept that whatever calamity that befell me was punishment for something I did wrong, or for someone else's wrongdoing (Eve? Adam?).

This model may or may not resonate with you and may not fit all situations, but it is a powerful example of how we can question and challenge accepted beliefs which may be imprisoning us, and to create our own models that suit us as individuals. As my teacher Natalie said, you can believe whatever you want, so why not believe something that will make you happy or give you meaning?

Each of these models provides a suggestion for how we can think about leaving. My thought is that we can pick and choose what we prefer, depending on what will help us most at the time. In the end, though, I view these models as having a common thread in that they all focus on our need for personal growth. Although leaving may be an undefined or non-specific part of each of these approaches, I interpret them as saying that sometimes leaving is a necessary step to our soul's freedom and to achieving our higher good. That's something I can get behind!

When I started asking people about leaving, everyone I met had a leaving story. Many of those are described further on in these pages, as you'll see. These stories helped me hone my ideas about the topic into this book. Some people responded with a bit of an attitude, saying, "I don't leave things, I *go toward* other things." I get that. But this book isn't so much about the 'going toward' part because of in many ways, the *going toward* is the easy part. It's less challenging when you see what you want and go toward it.

For example, perhaps you want to marry your very lovely fiancé. Perfect! So glad things are going well! But what are you leaving behind you? An identity as a fun, carefree single person? An identity as a lonely old maid or fussy bachelor? Freedom to do what you want? Isolation from your own family? A lifetime of wondering if anyone would ever love you? Even going toward something that is positive, you are leaving something else. Life is about making choices. And sometimes even the best choices bring a hint of sadness.

Note that although I am a leaver myself, I am not in any way advocating that leaving is the right choice for everyone all the time, or even for some people all the time. I advocate for thoughtful consideration of one's options, and then a leap into our destiny, whether that involves leaving or staying.

I love that process of identifying all the moving parts to these challenges and figuring out what to do right now. Of course, that may be because it makes financial sense, makes relational sense, is the *least worst* of several bad options, is just right in your gut ... however you make the decision, I suggest you make it thoughtfully and not let default mode move you forward. One of my biggest fears is that I'll wake up at 80 and wonder what happened to my life, so I do my best to militate against that feeling of "wasted time" by giving very careful consideration to all my major life changes.

Since I was a teenager, I've been writing down reasons for making big decisions. Perhaps because of my childhood of involuntary leaving, I wanted to document for posterity all the reasons for making big choices. Here's an example, from when I was 18: "Why are you joining the Army instead of going to college?"
- College is not financially sustainable for me right now.
- I think I would get bored at the universities where I was admitted.
- I need adventure, including signing up as an Army photojournalist to be stationed in Germany so I can travel overseas and learn new things.
- I really need to get away from home and become independent from my family; and
- The military provided funds for college, so I could do both.

I provided a few more details in my journal, but that is the gist of my reasoning. When I first looked back more than 25 years later, it was as if no time had passed, and every one of those reasons was still true. I'm so glad I kept those notes. Whenever I wonder about a decision

I made, I can review a snapshot of what I knew and felt at the time and my reasoning for leaving. Even if since that decision making moment I came across new information that might have influenced my decision had I known, I can review my thinking at the time and confirm that it is still valid. I have several of these documented experiences throughout my life, and the process of documenting has helped me increase my confidence that I am making good decisions.

Chapter 2: Who and What We Leave

Why are Americans in the middle of a leaving revolution? What do we leave?

- *We leave home*: Every spring, millions of 18-year-olds leave home to go to college, to join the military, or to move away from their parents and out on their own.

- *We leave jobs*: Typically, more than two million Americans leave their jobs every month – and even more during the Great Resignation, the widespread trend of workers quitting their jobs during the COVID-19 pandemic. Resignation rates increased on average by more than 20% during 2020 and 2021.[1] Four million Americans quit their jobs in July 2021 alone.[2] The Great Resignation is bucking traditional employment trends, with mid-level workers 30-45 years old (older Millennials and younger Generation Xers) leading the pack out the door. How employers respond to the Great Resignation is still unfolding, but clearly people are walking off the job in droves.

- *We leave spouses*: About 4% of Americans get divorced every year; in fact, the divorce rate among individuals in their 50s has more than doubled in the past 25 years.[3] Millions more break up with their boyfriends or girlfriends.

- *We leave a straight identity for a LGBT one*: Every year, teenagers and adults come out of the closet, leaving a straight identity to proudly assert their LGBT status. More than 4% of American adults now identify as LGBT, and more than 7% of Millennials.[4]

- *We leave religion:* Since 2000, the percentage of U.S. adults with no religious affiliation has more than doubled, from 8 to 19%, according to Gallup.[5] Half of Americans have changed their religious denomination at least once in their lives – many several times – while 28% switched faiths altogether (for example, from Christianity to Judaism).[6]

- *We let go of and move on from all kinds of other things too*: Many people start and then quit marathon training.[7] People drop out of high school, college, law school, medical school, and graduate school.[8] They drop out of therapy.[9] People refuse treatment and leave the hospital against the advice of their doctors,[10] and even quit life sustaining medical treatment.[11]
- *We even leave our country*: A *New York Times* article by Lana Bortolot[12] in 2020 highlighted the rise in people leaving the U.S. to become permanent expatriates, quoting figures from the U.S. State Department, which show that an estimated nine million U.S. citizens live overseas – a 47% rise from 2014.

We leave all kinds of things: Quitting and learning from failure has become a cause célèbre, including discussions in the *New York Times* and *Fast Company* (see For Further Reading).[13]

With all this leaving, it would seem we know what we are doing – but we don't. Little wonder that the top life stresses are:
- A spouse leaving (by divorce or dying)
- Leaving a job
- Leaving the single life/getting married
- Leaving one home for another

See a pattern?

Considering whether to leave, thinking through the options, and the actual process of leaving, are all extremely anxiety provoking. And, despite our shared ancestry of leaving – a collective history that makes leaving a common human occurrence – what do we really know about the process, how people make decisions to leave or stay, and whether leaving results in renewed growth and satisfaction? How can we measure its success? Do we even know how to leave in a way that is healthy and positive?

In interviewing more than a hundred people about their experiences of leaving and staying, I found that there were several common situations in which people struggled with leaving. There are other aspects of leaving that are rarer, but that can still cause anguish. The most common situations are outlined here.

Leaving home/family

Leaving our home and family is one of the most universal and most challenging forms of leaving we experience. For some of us, it's a gut wrench, pure and simple. For many of us, it is our symbolic transition to adulthood and the first major departure many of us undertake.

Historically, ceremonial or ritual transitions required young people to demonstrate that they were worthy of being treated as adults by their communities. For example, several Native American communities had a young person leave the tribe to spend time alone in the wilderness to face his fears, returning only when he has become a man (some tribes also had this process for women). Current U.S. culture, however, has relatively few shared rites of passage. Some cultures celebrate the transition to adulthood through quinceañeras, (celebration of a girl's 15th birthday culturally rooted in Mexico), bar and bat mitzvahs, first communions, or confirmations. Others view the arrival of adulthood with one's 18th birthday, of with various "firsts" such as first car, moving out, starting college, first time voting, first "legal" alcoholic drink, first job, getting married, having a child, or parents' passing. Regardless of how the transition from child to adult may be enacted, in many ways leaving home has become the last and most significant remaining "coming of age" rite. And even this rite of passage has become blurred, as between recessions and pandemics, young people are living at home well into their 30s. Some 52% of young adults under 30, around 26.6 million, were living with their parents in the U.S. as of July 2020.[14] This is in line with an upward trend since the 1960s, but the effect was increased by the pandemic and the related lay-offs and stay at home orders.

Leaving home has different flavors for different people. Some children go to boarding school and learn early on what it means to be separated from their families. Others stay at home until they are married, leaving only to move in with someone else. Some move into an apartment near their family and stay very involved with their families. Boarding school or college can be a way of easing into adulthood, possibly returning home during winter and summer breaks. Others leave to join the military as I did, where even though I was not old enough to drink, I was carrying a rifle to defend my country.

Developmentally, separating from our family and developing an individual sense of self, along with creating friendship networks and finding work, are the inter-related primary tasks of adolescence and young adulthood. These tasks are especially challenging given the key physical, emotional, social, and cognitive changes happening at the same time. Moving out of our parents' home and finding our way, however, is for many of us just one of many efforts to find out who we are. Of course, for many of us, leaving was not a big hug from parents dropping us off at a college campus. Leaving home may include running away to safety, moving towards a more dangerous life as I did in the military, or perhaps getting kicked out of our homes before being ready to leave.

Many times, the logistics of leaving home (such as finding a place to live, moving belongings, etc.) may overshadow the burden of the emotional transitions. Similarly, the parent's needs may sometimes make it challenging for the young person to manage the transition, such as if the parent is worried about the child's safety or is worried about their own identity without their child. This first leaving experience includes many bittersweet moments – a core aspect of many types of leaving. Mixed emotions are common, including excitement about moving onto the next step in life, fear about what is next, regret at leaving siblings or friends, conflict about leaving parents, feeling burdened by the weight of family expectations, or, conversely, free because there are no expectations ... This combination of feeling everything at once and being a little (or a lot) overwhelmed, can sometimes lead us to shut down and to float through the leaving experience on autopilot.

I was so happy when I left home. It was very liberating because my Irish-Catholic family was very domineering. My father couldn't understand why everyone didn't want to do things the way he did. When I left home to move from Manhattan to Brooklyn, you would've thought I was moving to Paris. But I was the baby leaving, which was a milestone for them.

-Tara (New York)

Regardless of how leaving home occurs, it's usually more than just a single moment. Typically, there are weeks, months, or even years spent planning to leave home. It's useful to think about how this process evolved:

- Do we choose to think of everyone's needs but ours?
- Do we focus firmly on our path forward?
- Do we pick fights before leaving, to relieve some pressure of the transition?
- Do we focus on logistics and not really communicate about our hopes, fears, sadness, and other feelings?
- How do we plan our moment of departure: sneaking off in the night, big blowout party with friends, low-key family get-together, or something else?
- Even if we leave on our own, do we celebrate the transition in some way?

- Do we congratulate ourselves on having the courage to take a leap?

How we leave home often becomes a template for how we manage leaving generally, so it's worth giving some attention to the points above.

Leaving a job

Who hasn't thought of leaving their job? Sometimes, the job we eagerly sought somehow finds its way under our skin and starts sucking out our soul day by day. Other times, we realize we no longer want to deal with our jerk boss, or that there's no advancement at this job, or that we're simply bored at work.

What leads us to take the plunge and start looking for something new? How do we balance the delicate process of maintaining good relationships with our bosses and co-workers while scanning the want ads at night? What about people who leave the rat race to become entrepreneurs, or those who are struggling to leave unemployment? And equally important, why do so many unhappy people stay in their jobs?

Although many baby boomers worked at the same organizations for forty-plus years and then either received a pension, received a buyout, or were laid off, later generations are now working at many more jobs over the course of a lifetime. This makes learning how to leave one even more important.

I worked three different jobs (two in retail) before I finished high school, and then was in the military. I had a series of time-limited traineeships while I was in graduate school that lasted a year or two, often part time, and eventually achieved various academic positions in universities. Each transition was a unique experience in leaving.

- I left a retail job because I was being sexually harassed (at 17!).

- I left the next retail job to join the military and earn money for college.
- In the military, I transferred several times from training to a permanent duty station, from one duty station to another, and then finally out of the military.
- I left a job because I felt conditions for the vulnerable adolescents in my charge were unsafe. (I was 22.)
- I left a job because working with incarcerated youths was too stressful and because I felt I didn't have the right skills and personality to be effective. (I was 23.)
- I left a job to move across the country with my spouse to be closer to his family.
- I left a job because there was no opportunity for advancement.
- I left a job because an ex I worked with made my life very difficult, especially after I got promoted over him.
- I left a job to start graduate school.
- I left another job because my boss was mean and insulting to everyone.
- I left a job because I felt I had accomplished what I set out to do for the organization.
- I left a job because it was time to move on to a new adventure.

I interviewed people who said they could leave their job, but only if there was a really good reason. They would ask, "How do you know when you've done enough so that you can assert that you've really given it your all?" My answer: you don't have to give it your all. You can just choose to leave if you want. I also talked to people who felt that leaving because you're bored is a perfectly valid reason to go.

We've all seen creative ways in which people leave their workplace. A disgruntled flight attendant engaged the emergency slide and slid right out of his job into freedom![15] Pamela Slim's 2009 book *Escape from Cubicle Nation: From Corporate Prisoner to Thriving Entrepreneur,*[16] outlines her thoughtful path from corporate worker bee to solo entrepreneur. A former colleague spent her last day at the office walking around with her phone playing the Disney movie song, "Let it Go," to the delight and annoyance of her co-workers. One of my favorite stories of creatively leaving a job is a colleague and friend who was fed up with the poor decisions his boss was making that were creating chaos in the organization. He confronted his boss and accused her of being mean-spirited and stupid. Her reply: "I'm not mean."

So why do people leave their jobs? Researchers have identified that when we leave our jobs voluntarily (not due to retirement, disability, or dismissal), we leave for two main reasons.

- First, we leave because we are dissatisfied with the job, with the organization, with inequity, with juggling roles, with a high-stress environment.
- We also leave because we think things will be better somewhere else, such as increased status, salary, or career development.

For many, there's a combination of both factors – first, the feeling that the current situation is not working, and second, the expectancy that the future will bring more satisfaction.

I left a full-time job because it came down to this: I was doing work I didn't want to do, with people I didn't want to do it with, geographically where I didn't want to be. Those three things together meant, "I need to get out."

-Eric (New York)

The "how" of leaving a job is often so stressful that many people prefer to remain miserable than to struggle with finding a new job, leaving the old one, and starting over with a new employer. The strain of leaving a job to become an entrepreneur has led to a cottage industry in advising how to make this transition (such as the excellent *Escape from Cubicle Nation* mentioned above). See Chapter 3: How We Leave – Six Steps to Leaving, and in Part 2 of this book you'll find useful tips for job-leavers (see Chapter 10: When Leaving Isn't Your Choice).

Leaving a romantic relationship
The decision to leave a relationship is not taken lightly. Breaking up happens in many ways but, typically, by the time we reach that decision, we will already have made substantial investments in the relationship. Initially, we may well get swept off our feet, and then naturally start to define ourselves, at least in some part, by our relationship. We enjoy the fun of being part of a couple. Sometimes, however, relationships can become stifling, boring, or even dangerous. It can be an extremely difficult decision to break up, especially when there are complicating factors – physical (living together), social (shared friends and in-laws), or legal (marriage, children, mortgage, wills) bonds.

What happens when the magic or satisfaction is gone? And how can we leave to start new lives?

Sadly, I have had this experience. I married the love of my life after a whirlwind romance, but after seven years, it became clear we wanted different things out of life and were no longer compatible. After I left, I checked out a book from the library: *Breaking Up is Hard to Do: Stories by Women.*[17] I spent a weekend devouring its 63 short stories about break-ups. Did I feel better after reading it? A little. The ice cream helped, too. But, as the book described in excruciating detail, breaking up is a terribly difficult process, and sometimes the only way is through it.

Sometimes breakups are because someone is moving faster than the other. One person has become stagnant while the other keeps learning.

-Anis (London)

As Paul Simon sang, there are indeed 50 ways to leave your lover. I've left romantic relationships because:

- We were not compatible in life goals or ambition.
- The other person was too aggressive and scared me.
- The other person was intimidated by me.
- The other person and I had physical intimacy approaches that were incompatible.
- The other person moved away, or I moved away.
- The other person was interested in a relationship, and I wasn't (and vice versa).
- The other person cheated on me and lied about it.
- The other person did not treat me well.
- The other person had hobbies or life perspectives or other activities that were not ones in which I wanted to participate.

Breaking up changes our brain structure as we attempt to accommodate the loss of the other person. It activates parts of our brain that are associated with physical pain (such as the anterior cingulate cortex, insular cortex, amygdala, and thalamus). Many daily activities also must be reconsidered, from the mundane of, "My partner always took out the trash," to renegotiating friend and family relationships, and sharing over and over that you are no longer together. These responses aren't gender neutral: research shows men tend to fall in love more readily, and women tend to fall out of love more readily.[18] Women are also more likely than are men to leave a relationship that seems ill-fated.

Leaving a partner isn't just leaving a person. It can mean leaving a best friend, lover, fantasy-sharer, complaint-listener, co-dreamer, co-parent, co-vacationer, and partner-in-crime for holiday parties, weddings, and family events. It's letting go of the idea that, "It's you and me against the world," or of someone always having your back. It's leaving the shared intimacies of the past, including falling in love, having children, and spending special moments together; leaving the shared friends, habits, and conveniences of today; and leaving the dreams for the future that you had created together. It's also leaving your annoying or insulting in-laws, petty squabbles, political differences, your partner's refusals to do chores, or the same arguments repeated over and over. Sometimes it means leaving behind cheating, lying, or abuse. It's wrapping all of that up and putting a lid on it.

When my ex-husband and I got married, we agreed to stay together if two statements remained true. First, each of us needed to feel that we were a better person together than we were apart, and second, we would stay together if we both wanted to keep trying. It was very sad when we realized that those were no longer true. But for the sake of our happiness – for our souls' purpose (although we didn't call it that at the time) – we made the very difficult decision to leave our marriage behind and begin separate lives. I don't regret getting married, and I don't regret getting divorced, even though it was painful. It has all been part of my journey.

I believe we must be free to pursue our own journey as the Hero of our own story. By "free" I don't mean free of a partner. I mean being with someone who not only lets you be you, but who also celebrates you, champions you, and cheers you on. Sometimes that gets complicated, like when one person wants to move and the other doesn't, and there must be compromise. Sometimes it becomes impossible, for example if only one partner wants a baby: there's no halfway with that. Leaving a partner is one of the most challenging forms of leaving there is because of how much we are intertwined with their lives. The steps described here can make it a little easier.

Leaving a home (moving)

As a veteran of 27 moves (counting only those where I stayed at least six months), I am an expert at finding a new place to live, purging "stuff," saying goodbye, packing up, unpacking, and exploring the new neighborhood. Moving is often associated with a new job, new spouse, or new city in a way that can compound the challenges of changing homes – and the adventure! The joy of moving has faded somewhat over the years; now I don't think it is particularly fun. But there is still a sense of adventure. The puzzle of the logistics of moving is still a valuable challenge – figuring out new stuff and building a new home with the energy and warmth I desire is fun to me. Knowing I can create a home wherever, whenever I want, that I can accomplish the move and stand on my two feet – this to me is priceless.

It's the first thing I think of when trouble comes – the geographic solution. Change your name, leave town, disappear, make yourself over. What hides behind that impulse is the conviction that the life you have lived, the person you are, is valueless, better off abandoned, that running away is easier than trying to change things, that change itself is not possible.

-Author Dorothy Allison in *Skin: Talking about Sex, Class and Literature*[19]

What leads people in the U.S. to move so much more than many other nationalities? Americans move an average of 11 times in a lifetime.[20] For most Europeans, it's closer to four (with exceptions for Finland and Norway, which are nearer U.S. rates). We move for clear and "acceptable" reasons – for college, for a job, for a better home, for a less expensive home, or because we're getting foreclosed upon or evicted. We also move for all kinds of other reasons that might not make sense to everyone or which might not seem like a "good enough" reason to move, such as boredom, or wanting to live somewhere else, or wanting to start over.

What are we looking for when we move? Moving is a hassle: finding a new place, packing up, renting or borrowing a moving truck, transporting everything and then collapsing amidst all the boxes in the new place. At the same time, moving because our family is growing, because we have a new opportunity across the country, because we can't take our upstairs neighbor moving furniture at 3 a.m. anymore, can have profound positive impact on our quality of life. Moving from one place to another takes a toll on our psyches, but it also opens worlds to seeing life differently. Our brains have literally to adjust to new geography, faces and routines in our new neighborhoods.

Packing for a move also makes us prioritize. It forces us to think about what belongings, what relationships, what habits are important. What do I really value? What did I value at one time but is no longer important to me? What can I let go of to make room for new things? Of course, this reassessment and reckoning is voluntary; we can instead choose to ignore the opportunity, throw everything in boxes and recreate the same process at the new home.

Some people can't imagine leaving their home. My aunt, for example, has lived in her home for more than 50 years. She raised her children there, knew the neighbors and their children their whole lives, and saw the neighborhood change with the decades. Now that she's widowed, her children asked if she wanted to move closer to them. Her answer: Absolutely not. She will never move. Even though I will never be that rooted to place, I admire that.

Melissa in New York, on the other hand, decided with her husband that they would buy a house in a new neighborhood because they needed a change. When I spoke with her, they had just bought the new house and were packing up their apartment. She said they were having second thoughts and were wondering why they were leaving their neighbors, the friendly proprietor at the corner store, and the restaurant with great pancakes two blocks away. But the more she talked about it, the more positive she became. She told me how much she enjoyed the fun of exploring a new neighborhood, making new friends, and developing new habits. "We needed a bit of a shakeup in our lives and didn't want to leave the city," she said. "It felt like we were doing the same thing over and over. It's hard to leave without a clear idea of where you're going, but it was just time to go. I'm excited about what's next."

Whether you move because of your neighbor, for work, or for adventure, moving is an intense experience that can uproot your sense of security and create a new and exciting life.

Leaving friends

Leaving a close friend, or being left by a close friend, can sometimes be more difficult than leaving a partner. We tell our best friends everything: our romantic relationships, our health issues, our parents, and our worries, fears, and insecurities. When a close friendship ends, it can be especially tough, especially if there is a feeling of betrayal or if the breakup splinters a group of friends. Two excellent story collections,[21] *My Other Ex: Women's True Stories of Losing and Leaving Friends*, Jessica Smock and Stephanie Sprenger, and *The Friend Who Got Away*, Jenny Offill and Elissa Schappell, (see For Further Reading) share gut-wrenching stories of friendship breakups. These breakups happened because of lives moving in different directions (especially with the arrival of children), misunderstandings, and for reasons never understood.

I have had several close friendships that didn't work out and where either I left, or they did. I left a close friendship after 15 years because our lives had moved in different directions and our relationship no longer felt comfortable. I had another friend who was also a work colleague. As we became more intertwined at work and I began to mentor her at her request, it became clear she was taking advantage of the friendship to not perform at work and to blame me for her choices. I had to back off from the mentoring relationship while fulfilling my professional obligations, and eventually I also left the friendship. Another time, I had a friend just stop talking to me. She said my divorce was hard for her and that my ex-husband and I were her model of how a couple could get along. She sent me an email saying she could no longer be friends with me and gave no other explanation. A few straight friends left me when I started dating women, and then a few gay friends left me when I dated men again. And, of course, I left friendships because I moved away, and it wasn't possible to bridge the distance and time.

I read somewhere that friends are in our lives for a reason, for a season, or for a lifetime. It's important to determine what you value in a friendship. My friend Phil told me his expectations for friends is that they are reasonable, considerate, fair, and honest; he has no problem ending friendships that do not display these qualities. This approach has made me feel better about the changing nature of friendships.

Leaving a religion

Many of us are raised with a strong attachment to our religion, and its culture is often tied into family events, celebrations, and milestones. Religion provides comfort, guidance, and consolation in many circumstances, not least of which is that it is a shared belief and value system with our family and our community. The term "religion" itself is from the Latin *re-ligios*, meaning "to tie together again." What, then, of those who leave their religion? How do individuals raised in highly religious families leave its religion? Where do they go, or what do they do next?

For many individuals, leaving the religion or denying God is deemed to be a very bad thing, leading to damage to one's soul and possibly to rejection by God. People struggle with letting go of the spiritual guidance they've received since birth. The experiences of those who have left religions, and their reflections on their identity and their spiritual well-being, provide rich material about leaving.

Some people leave the culture of the religion while maintaining beliefs, or vice versa. When I read published accounts of people leaving religions, whether Christian, Muslim, Judaism, or Mormonism, people who left tended to do so after a crisis of faith. These crises sometimes took the form of an eye-opening experience of abuse (financial, physical, or sexual) and finding the church leadership either less than sympathetic or actively hostile toward the victims. Author Martha Beck describes how her experience of childhood abuse was denied, and how her experiences were minimized or dismissed by the elders in her Mormon church, ultimately leading her to leave.

[Mormonism] was a kind of institutionalized madness, and its shackles were all the more confining for existing almost entirely in the human mind.

-Martha Beck in *Leaving the Saints* [22]

Not everyone has such an intense personal religious history, of course. Some people drift away from their beliefs in quiet apathy or disillusion, others make a more considered decision about their affiliation.

In his book *Leaving the Church: How I Lost my Faith Reporting on Religion – and Found Unexpected Peace*,[23] journalist and author William Lobdell begins by discussing his desire to join the Catholic Church when he started as religion editor for the *L.A. Times*. At first, he delighted in reporting on the joy and peace religion brought to many Los Angelenos. Yet, over time as his work lead him to investigate sexual abuse scandals, he also struggled to reconcile his desire to believe in Catholic tenets, and to join the church, with its response to abuse allegations.

It started to bother me greatly that God's institutions – ones He was supposed to be guiding – were more often corrupt than their secular counterparts. If these churches were infused and guided by the Holy Spirit, shouldn't it follow that they would function in a morally superior fashion than a corporation or government entity? In general, I was finding this wasn't the case. I started to see that religious institutions are more susceptible to corruption than their secular counterparts because of their reliance on God, and not human checks and balances, for governance.

-Author William Lobdell in *Leaving the Church*[24]

My own story was less dramatic. My mother grew up Syrian Orthodox, was baptized Roman Catholic, went to Catholic school, and got married in the Lutheran Church. When I was a child, we attended Baptist and Lutheran churches. As a small child, I remember attending a Sunday School class on Bible stories and asking why there weren't more women in the stories. Around 13 years old, I began my three years of weekly lessons to become confirmed as a Lutheran. I heard how Martin Luther nailing 95 theses to the church door became a symbol of the Protestant Reformation. I learned about early Christian men creating the Apostolic Creed of beliefs, then more men creating the Nicene Creed. As I understood it, women were excluded from all these processes and discussions about faith and beliefs yet were still expected to adhere to the faith and beliefs. As a teenager, while I grappled with rules about faith and ethical behavior, I became more and more convinced that the Church was created by men, about men, and for men as a way to maximize their interests, which included control of women. I also observed family members and fellow churchgoers, who from my perspective as an adolescent highly sensitive to hypocrisy, appeared to be less than "Christian."

By the time the confirmation ceremony was approaching, I was no longer in agreement with the Church's beliefs. I stopped going to church as soon as I left home.

Leaving for adventure

Some of us are driven to explore the world. Dreams themselves are often associated with travel, as our minds range outside of our bodies to learn about new places and events. Libraries and bookshops are full of stories about people who have struck out on adventures. Excellent leaving for adventure stories include John Steinbeck's cross-country road trip *Travels with Charley in Search of America*, Cheryl Strayed's best-selling memoir *Wild*, detailing her trek up the Pacific Crest Trail, William Finnegan's *Barbarian Days* on his surfing adventure, and Elizabeth Gilbert's global journey, *Eat, Pray, Love*.

John Steinbeck describes his itch to leave for adventure in *Travels with Charley in Search of America*:[25]

When I was very young and the urge to be someplace else was on me, I was assured by mature people that maturity would cure this itch. When years described me as mature, the remedy prescribed was middle age. In middle age I was assured that greater age would calm my fever and now that I am fifty-eight perhaps senility would do the job. Nothing has worked.

What leads us to head out on an adventure? Maybe we've always wanted to explore the country, either at home in the U.S., or further afield. Sometimes we may be propelled by a life crisis, such as a parent's death, or we may need to shake things up after divorce or redundancy. What happens when we are on the road? Do we get what we were looking for? And what were we looking for anyway? In my interviews with adventurers, I found that a combination of restlessness and a desire to "get away from it all" or to "reset" drives many adventurers.

Adventures give us space to be and to think unfettered by the regular ebb and flow of life responsibilities, such as job, household management, friends, co-workers, or family. This space is important for several reasons. First is the impact of just being in a space that is physically different from the usual habits of home, work, school, stores and so on. Have you ever been driving or taking the subway to work, and realize you've arrived after taking the correct turns automatically, without thinking about them? Adventuring puts you in a physically different space and has the impact of shaking out the well-worn pathways in your brain and forcing you to attend to your environment differently. Forcing you to think and see differently.

Adventuring gives one *space to think*. A nature trip gives plenty of space for solitude at natural vistas. In the big city, one can feel invisible walking down crowded streets. I know that not everyone leaves for adventure specifically to obtain space to think. Sometimes we leave for adventure with an intentional goal; for example, in my 30s, I took a solo road trip through Europe to heal from a breakup. But many times, it can be more amorphous. The topic that needs to be thought about might not be clear. In my experience, the beauty of leaving for an adventure is that adventuring provides space to let the mind wander through memories, dreams, imaginative possibilities, and to work itself out.

William Finnegan, after a childhood surfing in California and Hawaii, an English degree, and a job he loved, decided to leave on a surfing adventure to the South Pacific. In *Barbarian Days*,[26] he explained his reasoning:

I had five thousand dollars in the bank, by far the most I had ever saved. I was twenty-five, and I had never been to the South Seas. It was time for a serious surf trip, an open-ended wave chase. Such a trip felt strangely mandatory. ... In truth, difficult as it was, pulling up stakes was in many ways easier than staying. It gave me an excellent excuse to postpone mundane but frightening decisions about where and how to live ... I might even become another person – someone more to my liking – in the Antipodes.

Adventure also provides *space to be and grow*. Paths in our daily life can wear grooves we don't even recognize that over time, close us in and keep us tied to our habits. Similarly, our interactions with others (or our solitude) can create limitations that constrain us in ways we don't see until we've shaken up our routine. Adventuring can give space for us to act differently: to strike up a conversation with the stranger in the coffee shop in a way we never would at home or spend time with people we don't know.

Leaving one identity for another (married person, out gay person, city person)
Few events can provide such a profound shift in our lives as leaving one identity for another. Identity shifts often come with other changes, such as leaving singledom for marriage, leaving a closeted life to be an out gay person, or leaving one's hometown for the city (or leaving the city for the country or for another country). These are significant moves that require courage and resilience. They also change both how we see ourselves and how others see us.

Coming out was a substantial shift for me. Although there were lots of "should have known" moments, it all came together when I kissed a woman the first time. Aha! All that discomfort throughout my life was because I was gay! But … I wasn't an easy initial fit to the lesbian community. After dating a few women, I went back to dating a man. Then I determined that I must be bisexual. Then I started to have trouble with the "guy" part of being "bi". Then I fell in love with a woman. When she and I separated after seven years, after a while I dated a man.

At each juncture, I lost friends who disapproved of my actions and how I identified myself. Now I have created my own identity; I go with my own term that I created: "globally sexual." I concluded that everyone should have the opportunity and the challenge to figure out their own sexuality, rather than merely being born into a heterosexual default.

In addition to the challenges of preparing to change an identity, this kind of leaving comes with many repeated opportunities to explain oneself – which can be either affirming or annoying. Young gay men and lesbians often get to know each other by asking the two questions of, "When did you know you were gay?" and, "How did you come out?" Others ask

45

many questions about your decisions, requiring you to "come out" over and over about who you are and who you were.

In some situations, people view an aspect of your life as a part of your identity, even when you yourself don't see it that way. For example, I stopped talking about my military experience for a while because when people found out about it, they tended to view me as a "military person," rather than as a person who was in the military. Although I learned a great deal in the military, and was proud to serve, my veteran status is not a significant part of my identity some 25 years later. Upon learning I was in the military, people respond in ways that seem silly to me, like, "Oh, you being in the military explains why you're like this" (whatever *this* is). I grew tired of explaining repeatedly that I was "like *this*" before I joined the military, not because of being in the military.

My friend and women's history scholar Bonnie Morris writes about "coming out as a brainy girl." In her article, *A Different Bookworm: Coming Out, Brainy-Girl Style*,[27] Bonnie indicated that in many ways it was more challenging to "come out" as brainy than as lesbian. Bonnie said, "I could out-think adults around me. I felt that having that ability was by definition disrespectful. I learned how to be cute and cheerful because adults liked that better." Bonnie's article resonated with me quite a bit, and when I encountered situations that seemed to challenge my view of myself as a "brainy girl," I felt that my identity was being challenged and that I really wasn't all that great.

Many of us, especially women, have felt some version of "imposter syndrome" where we feel that we're not good enough, and that people will soon find out we don't belong in the job or degree. This sense of being unable to internalize our accomplishments and a constant fear of being exposed as a "fraud" can be debilitating.

Finally – and completely different from imposter syndrome – sometimes we forge new identities almost unwittingly, by instinct.

We may not consciously know what we're doing, but by following our inner urges, we may find they evolve into a new self, with new resilience.

I have been so frustrated with the political situation in Brazil that I really needed to leave. I decided I wanted to do something I've wanted to do for twenty years but I've always been too busy. I just ran away to Montreal for the summer to take a course and learn with people who think exactly how I do. It was perfect. When I came back to Rio, I had more patience to go back to work.

-Sandra (Rio de Janeiro)

Leaving behind a part of yourself
Sometimes what we want to leave is part of us. Deciding to change may mean abandoning a former version of ourselves. For example, in shamanism, clients and trainees often work on "deathing" aspects of ourselves that are no longer serving us. At a shaman training program, different people described what they wanted to "death":

- The part of me that regrets my decisions
- My fearful self: the part of me that is afraid to speak the truth
- The part of me that doesn't feel I'm worthy of having a place in the world
- The risk-averse me; I want to take more risks
- The person in me who doesn't hold myself and others accountable
- My belief that my wants are too much
- The part of me that doesn't believe I am enough
- The version of myself that is afraid to commit

All of these are parts of ourselves that have served us in some way – to protect us, to help us move forward, or to keep us safe. And for some shamans-in-training, these are parts of us that have persisted despite no longer serving our greater good. So it's time for those parts of ourselves to go.

I recently had an experience of leaving behind a part of myself that could not forgive. It was enormously cathartic to experience changing a long-time feeling of "I'm so angry at you," to feeling compassion and forgiveness. The process for letting go of these aspects in a shamanic context is beyond the scope of this book but is well worth exploring for individuals so inclined (See the For Further Reading section). There are so many parts of ourselves we can leave behind when we choose to, and the path is like the path of leaving home, leaving a job, or leaving anyone or anything else.

Leaving a path once chosen

Jae, a fantastic health services researcher, told me that she had once been on track to become a nun. She was a postulant for an order whose mission was to serve young women facing a life crisis. She was at the point of becoming a novice when her novice mistress (an older sister responsible for helping younger sisters join the community) suggested she take some more time to think deeply about her decision. Jae did, and as a result she came out as a lesbian and ultimately left religious life. She still remembers fondly her passion for Catholicism and her youthful idealism and is completely happy in the life she has chosen.

In an extreme example of abandoning a chosen path, some individuals leave a life as a criminal, gang member or a member of racist groups. Social scientists have studied "desistance" from activity in these groups and have identified factors that push individuals away from that lifestyle.[28] These include loss of belief in the ideology, social sanctions for belonging or believing, disillusionment with inner group workings, status changes within the group, exhaustion from persistent pressure and threat, and acts that were deemed too radical or extreme. Researchers have also noted the influences which pull this type of person toward alternative lifestyles, such as a desire for a conventional life, maturation, career opportunities and family responsibilities.

It is useful for this conversation to note that, more generally, many of us experience both these aspects of leaving a path – the elements that push us away from it, and those that pull us toward alternatives.

I remembered something I heard the author David Sedaris say in an interview once, which made me cheer: "Sometimes running away really works." You know what? Sometimes it really does.

-Author Elizabeth Gilbert[29]

I spoke to individuals who left their dream of becoming a lawyer to become a salesman, left a career in sociology research to become a rancher, and left corporate consultancy to become a shaman. As mentioned above, I spoke to someone who left her path to become a nun, and someone who left behind a life of crime. I spoke to people who left committed singledom to raise families. Who left their families to be alone. Who left interior design to become a yoga teacher. Who left work as a physician to become a rabbi.

There are substantial changes in lives that come with significant shifts in people's chosen paths. Such changes inevitably bring self-questioning. If the path we chose is no longer the right one, how can we trust our judgment about our next choice? What will we tell people who have always known us as someone who wanted to be a doctor, now that we really want to open a clothing shop, become a musician, or go travelling? Was becoming a doctor a necessary precursor to doing what we really want to do? These are important considerations and heady questions about what we want our lives to be. Who are we? What is our path? And how do we decide?

There are some common experiences and concerns when we think about leaving, whether it's leaving home, a relationship, a job, or anything else.

- How unhappy is unhappy *enough* to leave?
- How can I manage this logistically?
- What will my family/friends/co-workers/future employers think of this change, and how will they be affected?
- Will people be unhappy I'm leaving, and what are the consequences of that?
- How will leaving affect my life (career, prospects, financial stability)?
- How can I to continue struggle at this situation while looking for something better?
- How do I navigate awkward conversations repeatedly to let people know I'm leaving? How do I manage their emotional responses to my leaving?
- Am I ready to make a big change that affects everything?

There are also the hopes and excitement that what comes next after leaving will be better in some way: more fulfilling, more exciting, less harmful. Or even a sense that we're not sure what's next, but we can no longer do *this*. That's okay too. Next we will review the stages of leaving, in which we have the opportunity to consider these profound questions.

Chapter 3: How We Leave: Six Steps to Leaving

There are as many ways to leave as there are things and people to leave. From heartfelt discussions to walk out on a marriage, to quitting a job by leaving a post-it note, we all have our own style. In my interviews and in my own experience, I found that many people struggle with whether to leave, how to leave, and how even to *start* thinking about the possibility of leaving. Many people become paralyzed at different points in the process, and the anxiety is real. It's a sad fact that many people are willing to stay unhappy for a long time, yet, often, their fears and anxieties prove not as difficult to overcome as they initially thought. It may help to know that there are certain steps that are common in leaving situations.

This chapter describes six steps that emerged from interviews and other research. Of course, not all of these happen in every leaving situation. Sometimes, things happen so fast that there's not much time for them. Leaving, after all, is a form of identity development (more on that later). When we are accorded the time and circumstances to consider thoughtfully the prospect of leaving, however, these steps typically accompany our considerations. These steps are each described in greater detail in Part 2.

Six steps to leaving
1. Awareness
First, there is an *awareness* that one's situation is somehow in itself harmful to one's being, whether it is abusive, inhibiting growth (ours or others'), unsatisfying, or merely boring. This is like the first step in the Hero's journey, where we start to see ourselves in the context of our upbringing, our current circumstances, and everything that brought us to this point. The importance of this developing awareness cannot be overstated. Awareness that there are other possibilities in life, something else one might have been called to do, is powerful.

This can be a painful process initially. The temptation to resist change can be strong. But, after the first pangs of discomfort, realizing that change is possible can be a huge relief. Increasing our awareness that things could be different is often tied in with *hope*, a sense that leaving will make them not just different, but better. This hope starts to coalesce the possibilities. We make an honest assessment of our current situation and determine that there is hope for a better life by removing ourselves from our current situation.

Many of us go back and forth imagining different scenarios in our heads about what life could be like. If I did *x*, would life be better? What if I did *y*? Will our financial situation improve, will we feel safer, will our children be better off, will I finally be happy?

The Buddha said that just as you can recognize seawater because it always tastes of salt, you can recognize enlightenment because it always tastes of freedom.

-Martha Beck, *Leaving the Saints*[1]

Awareness is changed by hope, and vice versa. Once we become aware things could improve if we go, there is a reality that some things will get worse, or not change — or that if we go, things will become worse for others we care about. This may make us want to shut down our awareness and just give up and accept things as they are. Plenty of situations provide opportunities for leaving, where the answers aren't clear, such as whether to take a job across the country that will uproot our family. These same issues can lead us to *not* leave – not leave home right now, not go on the adventure, not try to work it out with a partner.

In these situations, as psychiatrist and author Viktor Frankl wrote,[2] when we can't change the situation, we are challenged to change ourselves. Chapter 4: Awareness, further discusses how we may resist this initial awareness that things could improve if we leave, along with what to do next.

2. Confidence

Once possibilities are identified, we must develop *confidence* about leaving. We must determine that whatever lies ahead is something that we can face, that we can deal with, and that will ultimately be better than whatever was left behind. There is much we can do to increase our confidence, including recognizing our own accomplishments, obtaining encouragement, and observing and interviewing others who have been successful. We will explore this further in Chapter 5: Confidence.

3. Decision

The decision to leave can be sudden, slow, or an iterative process where you make and unmake the decision many times. I propose a thoughtful and logical process to think through possibilities, while also acknowledging that many times, you must follow your intuition. The logical process prepares you to take the leap when the time is right. Sometimes, though, things come together in a way that seems like magic and that propels you into leaving.

Imi, a former factory worker in Romania, knew that emigrating to the U.S. would lead to a better life. He knew his parents supported his emigration even though they would likely struggle after he left, since he was their only child. He explained that two incidents that happened the same week solidified his decision to leave.

First, a man was put in charge of our group at the factory only because he had a rich father. He didn't know anything about the factory, and we had to teach him everything. This struck me as such an injustice, which is saying a lot after many, many injustices in Romania. I told a friend of mine about this injustice. My friend told me that if I really wanted to leave, he could get us visas to the U.S. if we signed on to work for a moving company. This was the path I was looking for! It was incredible how the injustice at the factory led me to find the exact path I needed to leave Romania for the U.S.

-Imi (Washington DC)

Chapter 6: Decision, walks us through how to decide when you have the time to think it through.

4. Preparation

There may or may not be *preparation* for the departure, which could involve logistics, packing items, transitioning relationships, and getting mentally ready for what lies ahead. Although many people struggle with the logistical concerns, arguably the most important preparation is internal and mental. Two additional areas of consideration in the preparation stage are the opportunities to consider how open we should be with others, and how to garner support from friends, colleagues, and loved ones. Would it make sense to tell many people about leaving? If not, are there safe people we could share with who would provide support and encouragement – or perhaps add a critical different perspective? Are there mentors who can guide the way and provide advice? Chapter 7: Preparation, discusses the down and dirty about preparing to leave – both the logistics and the emotional aspects.

5. Leaving

The *leaving* itself is the big push where we gather up our resolve and take the step that moves us further into our future. This is the point that our awareness, our hope, our confidence, and our planning gather up in a storm and propel us forward. It's an emotionally powerful step toward the rest of our lives. Regardless of how the leaving takes place, in the moment of leaving, you may feel unreal, unsettled, or as if you are hanging on a precipice. That's okay: it's normal. Being able to tolerate feeling unsettled while moving forward is a sign of strength. Chapter 8: Leaving, discusses the actual leaving itself, what people experience when they leave, and how to enjoy the ride (or manage the tumult). (Hint: It will all be just fine.)

6. Integration of leaving into your life story

Finally, once we have begun the journey and start to *integrate the past and present* in our life stories, there may be varying levels of nostalgia, guilt, or ennui. Whatever was left behind could be considered a challenge we triumphantly overcame, a guilty secret from a shadowy past, or something we never talk about that our new friends and colleagues might never suspect.

I have documented my reasons for leaving in case I ever have doubts. Only a few times have I returned to review what I was thinking at the time, and each of those times I was instantly reassured that I had made the right decision. In fact, I believe we all make the best decisions we can with the information we have. At first, I was ashamed of how frequently my family moved, and I felt embarrassed I kept on leaving homes and jobs. It's taken many years for me to integrate each of these leaving experiences into a narrative whole, and that story is not that my family and I are flawed because we have moved so frequently. My story is that I have a keen sense of when things are not working for me, I'm willing to take risks to make major change to be happy, and I am an adventurer. Chapter 9: Integration, describes how to integrate your experience into your story.

Leaver or stayer?

My interviews taught me that many of us identify ourselves as either leavers or stayers.

Leavers are those of us who tend to move around in our relationships, living situations, and jobs. Many of us leavers have at least several moves under our belt as kids, and we have an acute awareness of what it's like to be uprooted and must make new friends and figure everything out from scratch. We don't know what it's like to have lived in the same place all our lives, or to have friends who knew us when we were young. Similarly, we're not afraid to uproot ourselves as adults. Some of us get restless and start feeling trapped and uncomfortable if we go too long without a major life change.

There are also those of us who grew up leavers who become stayers, or who grew up stayers and become leavers. Chapter 12: If You Can't Leave, addresses whether we can really change our spots, along with those who would love to leave but are afraid or overwhelmed at the prospect. There are those who would love to stay but can't seem to, because when the restlessness gets in our bones, we have to be moving on. Leavers and stayers both have strengths and weaknesses, of course. We all have our own struggles.

I'm fascinated with the concepts of leaving and staying. I love that people tend to know immediately whether they're leavers or stayers. Yet, although leaving and staying is such a central part of our lives, nearly everyone I interviewed said they hadn't really thought about their lives in these terms. While I am a leaver, I'm not always pro-leaving – indeed, I wrote this book so I could better understand my own patterns of leaving and staying. And to help others leave or stay, whichever is right for them.

Part 2

Chapter 4: Awareness

I try to leave a job when I'm on top. I don't want to wait until I'm unhappy. That way people always remember me as awesome.

-Marie (Arizona)

The first step in leaving is the development of an awareness that things could be better than they are– even if it seems far-fetched way or impossible right now. There may be a realization that one's situation is somehow harmful to one's being, whether it is abusive, inhibiting growth (ours or others'), unsatisfying, or merely boring. I picture this happening as a glimmer of light in the darkness that flickers dimly and then is usually put out quickly. Over time, we go back to that light, poking at it, playing with it, until hopefully it becomes brighter and more real. Sometimes, though, we are so scared at the initial light that we just cover it up and it eventually goes out.

First glimmer of awareness
Imagine you are unhappy at your job, as are many people. Maybe you don't like your boss, or you feel you're not being paid enough, or you've outgrown your job, or you just want to do something entirely different. Whatever the reason, you know you have been unhappy for a while, but it didn't occur to you to leave your job. Then somehow it comes up. Maybe a friend mentions she is happy at her job, or your spouse says, "Wow, sounds like you're really unhappy," or you look around in a meeting and think, "I really could do better." You may have thought those things before, but this time there's just the right spark. It suddenly feels like a real possibility, not just griping or

complaining. That little light appears with a whisper of "What if?" or "Maybe" or "Perhaps." I love that light. The glimmer of possibility is a gorgeous thing. It can also be scary.

As a child of divorced parents, I learned early about breakups. I grew up hearing my mother's story. In the 1970s with two toddlers, my mother suspected my father was cheating on her. She prayed for a sign to confirm her suspicion, and asked God to hurt him, just a little, if he was cheating. He came home that night having caught a fishhook in his finger: she knew. She had been putting money away from the "allowance" he gave her just in case. Back then, that was not uncommon, at a time when women couldn't get credit without their husband's approval. My first knowledge of breakups: one person is at fault, and you're lucky to make it out alive.

Extinguishing the first glimmer
A first reaction for many of us is to extinguish that light with all kinds of reasons why it's just not possible. Here are some thoughts you might have if you're just starting to think about leaving a job:
- My current job's not *that* bad
- I like my colleagues
- The work is okay
- What if I can't find another job?
- I'm worried about finances
- What if leaving here damages my career?
- People will be upset if I leave
- I don't want to lose my pension
- I don't have time to look for another job
- No one else could do my job
- I earned seniority and don't want to go back to being new again
- I'd hate to leave my staff/boss/colleagues/customers
- It would be difficult to transition to a new job
- What if another job is worse?

Do any of these sound familiar? It's natural to let all of those worries and concerns take over and push the thought a new job out of your head. "Pssht! What was I thinking, a new job? I have my hands full right now. That was a crazy idea..."

I'm here to tell you that it's okay to do that. It's okay to muffle that spark and drown it in a sea of negative thinking – at least temporarily. I get that the glimmer is scary. *Of course* it's scary. You're having initial thoughts about a major life change! And our example here is "just" a job, whereas it could be leaving home, leaving a spouse, leaving the country ... things that could evoke even more fear. The challenge is when you don't go back to it and truly see what's happening. If you see this happening, let it be for a little bit. Allow yourself to be scared for a while. Recognize that you had a spark and shut it down. And wait for it to come back again, because ...

The glimmer returns

... That spark is still there. That awareness is still there that maybe, perhaps, possibly there is something else. So perhaps a week later, or a month, that spark shows up again. And this time you're a little slower to quash it down. Maybe this time you think, "I really am unhappy, and I really don't like the work, but ... I don't have time to look for another job, no one else could do my job," (or pick another reason from the list above). This time, hopefully it's a little less scary. You're a little slower to completely squash it. It's okay to squash it again (no judging!) but this time, try to take some notes before you put out the light. Try to identify both what the spark is (changing jobs or changing something else?) and what it is that makes you shut it down. You might come up with a list like the above. Identify what's on that list. Write it down, or log it in your head, so you can come back to when it's less scary. It might take several iterations until you have a clear sense of what the spark is and what's on your shut-it-down list.

Examine your shut-it-down list

Once you're ready with a solid list, it's time to look at it. I know it can be scary. You can do this. Here's the time to play a game called "examine the evidence." I'm showing my psychologist roots here: this is a technique used in cognitive-behavioral therapy, which I feel is useful to consider in the form of a game. The idea is to get comfortable just thinking things through. There's no need to make any decisions right now!

Start with an easy item on your list, such as, "I shouldn't leave because my job's not that bad." Start asking yourself questions to get to the evidence of that statement yourself. For example:

- So how bad is your job, really?
- How do you feel when you go to work? Do you get heartsink as you enter the building? Or do you feel energized and uplifted?
- How do you want to feel when you go to work?
- Where would you rate this job on a scale of 1-10, with 1 being the worst job in the world for you and 10 being the best job in the world for you? Is that score okay with you?
- What is it about your job you like?
- What do you not like?
- How important are the not-likes and the likes?

The point isn't to definitively determine if "my job's not that bad" is true or false, because that's not possible. It's to determine if these individual reasons for not changing are actually true. My hunch is they might not be.

Let's try another one. "I shouldn't leave because I like my colleagues."

- Who are the colleagues I like?
- Would leaving mean I would never see them again?
- Would it be possible to maintain a relationship with them if I'm working somewhere else?
- If some relationships didn't continue beyond a move, how bad would that be?

- Is "liking my colleagues" a good reason to stay at a job I don't like?

These are just for starters – I invite you to think up more.

Whatever your shut-it-down statements, tackle them! It may be that you end up deciding that your statements are true, that you like your job, and you don't want to leave. That's fine. Or that you don't like your job, but it's not time to leave. That's fine, too. But since that awareness came into your head, look at it, go with it, play with it, investigate it. Turn it over and look on the underside and stretch it and see what's true and what's not true. Consider what makes you uncomfortable or anxious. Think about what you would feel comfortable sharing with friends, versus what you don't want to tell anyone.

Consider this process in the context of your life

We've all met people who have made themselves too small for their lives, where there is so much more they could do. This next step encourages us to look beyond ourselves. Jungian analyst James Hollis, who writes about challenges in mid-life, calls this "stepping into largeness."[1] It's like the first step in the Hero's journey, where we start to see ourselves in the context of our upbringing, our current circumstances, and everything that brought us to this point. This increased awareness of a need for change may start with a casual comment from someone else that makes us think about ways in which our life could be different, or something that has never set well with us. It could start with pursuing a growing sense of "something's not right," or finally having the courage to pursue that part of our soul that is not happy with where things are.

Stepping into largeness doesn't always involve leaving, but it certainly could. When you consider your life to this point, is leaving an opportunity to step into largeness?

The importance of this developing awareness cannot be overstated. Awareness that there are other possibilities in life — something else one might have been called to do — is powerful. Although this may happen at mid-life, it can strike any time, and cause us significant discomfort. It may challenge our identity significantly, for example if the idea of leaving a spouse contradicts the family rules that people don't get divorced in *our* family. Leaving a job may arouse financial fears. It may suggest social exclusion, such as leaving one's hometown for college. Awareness of a different path may prompt self-critical thoughts and worries that we have been on the wrong path all this time. Don't believe it. We are on the right path; awareness of a different path couldn't have happened unless we followed the path we were on.

Questions we have may include:
- Could there really be something different?
- Maybe I'm misreading this calling?
- Could I ever *really* make that change?
- What will people think?

We might also feel fearful and wish to deny the awareness.

As well as a potential job change, the same process can be applied to any other areas you're dissatisfied with, such as home, a partner or a neighborhood. Use your questions to grow that spark and really look at the light to see what's there. There's no need to change a single thing in your life while we play this game. This is just thinking. Meanwhile, you're developing and clarifying your awareness.

Katrina said that at 31, she was happy being a stayer in her hometown of San Antonio. She had a full-time job at the local news station, and she listened to live music and went dancing on weekends with her friends. She described a turning point when a stranger in a bar started an argument.

He had traveled abroad and was telling me about it. I was genuinely interested, but at some point, he turned on me. He started saying I needed to get out and experience life outside of San Antonio, but he said it in a really insulting way. He said I wasn't living, and that I hadn't lived until I wiped my butt with a leaf. He made me feel like my life was worthless. I felt like I was having to defend my life. He was really insulting, and finally the bartender kicked him out. He made me angry, but that argument made me start thinking about what I really wanted out of life. Yes, I was happy, but was I really fulfilling my potential? The argument spurred me on to think about leaving San Antonio to fulfill a dream of working in television in New York City. Less than a year later, my friend and I planned our big move to NYC at that same bar.

Sometimes that initial glimmer of awareness is not a feel-good glimmer. Do you remember what it was like to be a teenager? Many of us yearned to be a grown-up and have opportunities that were denied us as children – only to realize, too late, how free childhood is.

In *Wild*, Cheryl Strayed describes a series of life experiences that were like successive punches in the gut, leading her to leave for the adventure of a thousand-mile hike on the Pacific Coast Trail. Her mother died of cancer, she got divorced, terminated an unwanted pregnancy, and then drifted aimlessly. When she was feeling at her lowest, she described her Aha! moment when she said to herself, "*I had to change. ...* Not into a different person, but back to the person

I used to be – strong and responsible, clear-eyed and driven, ethical and good. And the PCT would make me that way."[2]

Sometimes at this point we decide to stay. We do not want to go further. Although I encourage going through the steps, there are times when this is an approach that makes sense for us.

My family had the possibility to move to Singapore for my husband's job. We checked it out as a formality, but I couldn't do that to my kids. My mother grew up in rural Alabama and was the first to integrate her school. I'm sure she was picked because she was smart, pretty, and well spoken. She didn't want to go, and it was a hostile experience, but her father was very insistent that she succeed. Later with me, I tested well and was sent to a different school for smart kids. There was no one who looked like me. It exposed me to a different world, but it was hard. I learned cruelty at an early age. I am sure I would not have become a chemical engineer without that experience, but I just couldn't put my kids through that. We decided not to move to Singapore.

-Nikkia (Atlanta)

Some of my favorite opportunities to leave for adventure – the situations that anticipated the glimmer – were precipitated by breakups or life changes. For example, I was finishing school and several hoped-for job opportunities evaporated, all in the same week! I was facing a mortgage with no job, so I inexplicably booked a month-long trip to India to coincide with the end of training. It worked out perfectly in the end: when I was sitting in a tiny Internet café in New Delhi, I received an email informing me I had a new job.

I probably won't stay in Connecticut for three reasons, which emerged recently. First, my nostalgic reasons for staying are gone. I came back to Connecticut to work with my father and take on the world and to be with my family. Those were personal reasons. My father passed away and my mother moved away, and now it's just work. Second, my logical reasons for staying at the business are gone. I know I've topped out what I can do at that company. ... I grew it ten times from what it was to what it is today. Literally all I'm doing now is making it so I don't have to be there in person. That's not the right way to be when you're trying to grow a business. Finally, my priorities in my personal life have changed. When I started I was 23. Now I'm 35. I want a wife and kids, and they will be my number one priority. Then I couldn't have my business be my number one priority. All that's keeping me here in my hometown is the job. I don't have to stay. And I don't want working and living in the same bubble to define who I am.

-Agung (Connecticut)

The important thing to do at this stage is to sit with it. Of course, if there is immediate danger, it's important to move quickly to safety. But for those of us who have the luxury of time and who are safe, it's important to take the time to just experience those feelings and let our brain chew on them without judgment. It's also important to give ourselves time to explore the awareness that something could be different without immediately clamping down with a need to act. We should not be driven by anxiety or judgment. That judgment might not even be ours: it may be the judgment of everything we've been taught, which doesn't necessarily reflect the individual in us struggling to become free.

Allow yourself to feel hopeful

As you're considering these life decisions, it's important to allow yourself to feel hopeful. Hope consists of two parts: a desire for an outcome, and a belief in the possibility of that outcome. Our new awareness has started us off on a desire for an outcome, even if right now that outcome is vague and only defined as "something better." We will work on clarifying that outcome. For now, we will focus on the second part, a belief in the possibility of an outcome. This step is focused on moving from a glimmer of possibility that things can get better, to a belief that change *will* make them better.

Hope has long fascinated philosophers and storytellers. When all the evils escaped from Pandora's Box, only hope remained. Why did hope remain? To keep hope *from* humans, or to ensure hope is available *for* us? There is also much discussion about whether hope is good (a comfort, an encouragement) or not (a distraction from reality). Philosopher Aristotle encourages us to use our hope to pursue the noble.[3] St. Augustine suggests hope is what allows us to be truly virtuous citizens.[4]

No surprise to anyone considering leaving, hope is often accompanied by fear and anxiety. Seneca describes hope and fear as marching in unison like a handcuffed prisoner and escort.[5] By its nature of looking into the future, hope keeps our minds in suspense and, sometimes, in a state of anxiety. Descartes, however, assures us that hope is worth it.[6] Hope also underlies the more complex passions of boldness and courage. Even famously negative Nietzsche calls hope "the rainbow over the cascading stream of life"[7] – although in true Nietzsche fashion, he could just mean hope is illusory and quick to fade; he also calls hope the worst of all evils, so go figure. Psychologist Charles

Snyder proposes that hope is the process of thinking about one's goals, along with the motivation to move toward (agency) and the ways to achieve (pathways).[8]

John Steinbeck planned an American road trip chronicled in *Travels with Charley in Search of America* because he had hope that he could learn about America and that the experience would help him become a better writer:

For many years I have traveled in many parts of the world ... but I discovered that I did not know my own country. I, an American writer, writing about America, was working from memory, and the memory is at best a faulty, warpy reservoir. I had not heard the speech of America, smelled the grass and trees and sewage, seen its hills and water, its color and quality of light. I knew the changes only from books and newspapers. But more than this, I had not felt the country for twenty-five years. In short, I was writing of something I did not know about, and it seems to me that in a so-called writer this is criminal. ... So it was that I determined to look again, to try to rediscover this monster land.

-John Steinbeck[9]

How you hope and what you hope for can include the idea of what you feel you deserve from life. What kind of life do you want? What would "stepping into largeness" look like for you? What do you want to accomplish by the end of your life?

Some people think they don't deserve much. We've all had moods where we feel the best we can hope for is to eke through life with little joy other than chips and television. Some people feel safer with lower expectations. They may feel that people are going to be disappointing just by their nature, that things aren't going to go their way, and that pessimism (which they cleverly disguise by calling it realism) is a good approach because then they'll be disappointed less frequently. They may feel they will never live up to their ideals if they dream big. In this way, lack of hope can be protective. They believe reality has not been kind to them, and they suffer because of it. At various stages of our lives, we may identify with this to a greater or lesser degree. Regardless of what your past experiences have been, what do you hope for? What are your greatest dreams? Would leaving move you closer to those dreams?

At a conference, I was partnered up with Paul from North Carolina. Our assignment was to discuss a current challenge in our lives. Paul told me that his dilemma is that he and his girlfriend have a good relationship. I wasn't sure how to interpret this – it didn't sound like a problem. He said the challenge is that at 28, they were pretty settled in together, with a good relationship and they have things to talk about and some common interests ... but there was no excitement. She wasn't ambitious like he was, and there were areas of disconnect as well. He also really loved her and said she loved him. He said she would be devastated if he broke up with her, and that everyone in their extended families and friend circles would be shocked. He said his dilemma was that he didn't know whether to give up a good relationship in search of a great relationship, or to settle for a good relationship.

Paul's dilemma gets to the crux of hope. Should we leave what we have – with its strengths and weaknesses – in hopes of finding something better, or should we stick with what we know? Should we hope for better, and possibly risk getting something worse, or make do with what we have? And does leaving mean we have lost hope that things will get better if we stay?

Another companion to hope and fear is shame. The hope that things will get better, the fear they won't, the shame that we screwed up by aiming too high or by throwing away something that was good. Some people live in fear of making the wrong decision — to stay or to go. Others associate fear with both decisions — if I stay, then this bad thing will happen; but if I go, this other bad thing will happen. Or they are just unable to act. And the whole process is covered in shame. What a bind we put ourselves in sometimes! The good news is that our brains generally like action. Taking action to make a positive change tells our brains that we are actively *doing something* to make our lives better. That's a good thing.

I think people who leave are really fearful that their current situation won't work out, so by leaving, they don't have to see if they would have failed if they had stayed. And stayers get to feel good about staying without fearing that if they went out and left, they would fail in their leaving.

-Andrew (New York)

Susan Jeffers, author of the fabulous books *Feel the Fear and Do it Anyway* and *Embracing Uncertainty*,[10] describes fear as a lack of trust in your ability to handle whatever comes your way. Building this confidence (addressed in the next chapter) greatly reduces fear because anything you choose is a No-Lose Situation. Shamans suggest we feel fear in everyday life when we forget that everything is unfolding exactly as it should. Fear and shame are intertwined in several ways.

Shame about wanting to move on. People often feel bad because something isn't working out, as if they could or should be able to control everything. There are of course opportunities to make our lives better in a myriad of small and large ways. Women often feel bad for leaving when they are unhappy or oppressed or bored or not learning any more, according to women's history scholar Bonnie Morris. "Women aren't supposed to be ambitious, so we often carry a lot of shame baggage when we think of leaving. But if there's so much more we could be doing, we're often called too ambitious or a workaholic. I don't think I'm a workaholic – I think I'm living up to my potential."

Agung said similarly, "People will think you're ungrateful to leave something they think is good, but just because you're well off doesn't mean you're happy. You can choose to weigh happiness as an intrinsic spiritual value more than reputation, status, or financial security. I think it's important that once we're no longer in survival mode we can focus on higher levels of being."

It's natural to feel some shame because you're ready to move on, whether it's from a job, home, religion, partner, or friendship, but it's not necessary. You can feel happy you had the experience, and sad it's ending, and you can move on without the shame.

Shame about leaving people behind. "You can't save everyone." How many times have I been told this? Sometimes our desperation and frantic sense of self-survival leads us to make decisions that we might later regret. In a New York Times Magazine article in 1995 by Alexis Jetter,[11] author Dorothy Allison says of her escape from poverty in North Carolina: "The thing about working-class escapees is that they leave others behind. Neither of my sisters graduated from high school … Well, honey, at twelve I was ready to flush them down the toilet for a chance to get out, and I pretty much did."

You can conduct a reasonable assessment about who you might be able to save or bring with you, and you can do your best to help them become self-sufficient in your absence. Or you can be like the airplane emergency instructions: Secure your mask first before you help others.

Shame that leaving means you failed. I heard this concern quite frequently from the people I interviewed. I have personally felt this shame about leaving relationships and about leaving jobs. I felt helpless, thinking, "I'm trying everything I can but it's still not working!" But remember that sense of omnipotence we sometimes want to pretend we have? It's not possible for one person to be fully responsible for both sides of a relationship. Each person can — if they choose — do their best and take responsibility for their own actions and feelings and responses.

I am eternally hopeful. However, I do eventually learn when it's not working, and I need to do something differently. My rope is much longer than I ever thought it was in trying to make things work, but eventually I may still reach the end of it. And that's when I really need to figure out what I'm going to do. Having hope that the next step will work out well is helpful – even essential – at this point.

I've seen so many people stay miserable in jobs because they have kids in college, or they don't want to give up their lifestyle, or they are simply afraid. And, believing there are no other options, they stay miserable at their work! So many of those people think we are all in the same boat they are, that we are making the same decision to be miserable because we feel we have no other choice. They haven't met people who don't really need others and who aren't willing to stay in the same place. It doesn't necessarily mean you have to leave your job and throw your whole life up in the air – it could mean moving sideways, or into a different game altogether.

As Agung said, "Courage is when you don't know the outcome, but you still want to make the same decision."

The bad news is that sometimes leaving doesn't necessarily resolve the situation of shame and fear. *But it will have been worth it.*

In summary, the first step in leaving is an awareness that things could possibly be better if we left some situation. Our mind usually reacts to this first glimmer of awareness by trying to shut it down. Careful examination of our fears and concerns, as well as allowing ourselves to feel some hope, while hopefully minimizing shame and fear, can help move us forward in considering whether leaving is right for us. The next chapter discusses the second step in leaving, developing confidence that we can do this. (Hint: we can!)

Chapter 5: Confidence

It's important to have confidence. I really think that's what people fear: that something will come along, and they won't be able to handle it. I have been through some difficult [leaving] situations, and I know now that there's nothing I can't handle.

-Charles (South Africa)

Confidence is hot. But it's hard to feel sexy when you feel like the world is on your shoulders, and you're trying to make (what seems like) the most important decision of your life. If you feel overwhelmed, it means it's time to back away slowly and take a deep breath. Confidence is a choice we make. Sometimes it's a simple if-then statement. If I make x change, then y will get better. If I graduate from college, then I'll likely make more money. If I break up with my boyfriend, I'll feel better about myself. But sometimes it gets worse first (college takes effort, we feel sad after a breakup), and you don't usually know how much worse things will get. How do you develop confidence to make a change?

I see confidence in the context of leaving as a three-part process that integrates (a) the hope things will get better if we leave, (b) the belief we will be able to handle whatever comes our way, and (c) the conviction that, regardless of how it works out, taking the chance will have been worth it. We discussed hope in Chapter 4, *Awareness*. This chapter discusses how to clarify what you're looking for, how to believe you can handle what comes your way, and a discussion of whether taking the chance will be worth it.

I think many people are scared to leave. They'd rather live with the mess they know than to go out in the world and encounter some scary stuff. But you can always make it through the scary stuff.

-Sue (Seattle)

What are you trying to accomplish?

Confidence is more easily developed when you consider what exactly you want to accomplish and what your options are. When you're thinking of leaving, what is it exactly you think will be better? Typically, it's that you will have less of something bad and/or more of something good.

For example, you may want to:
- Leave a job to have less stress
- Leave a spouse to have less resentment
- Leave an educational program to have less boredom and frustration
- Leave a neighborhood to have less expense and hassle

You may also want to:
- Leave a job to make more money
- Leave a spouse to have more happiness and contentment
- Leave an educational program to have more freedom
- Leave a neighborhood to have more disposable income and ease of functioning

What is it you want to accomplish? Once you've decided that, it might be helpful to think about two key questions: How likely it is that leaving the situation will result in more or less of what you'd like? And are there other ways to get what you want that might be just as good if not better than leaving?

Nearly nine months before I actually broke up with my girlfriend, I considered it but didn't have the confidence. I was visiting friends that I knew only from the Internet. I remember spending a week with them and thinking to myself: "Wow, these people who don't know me and don't have a stake in my life at all are treating me better than my girlfriend of five years. Why am I putting up with how she treats me? They think I'm amazing and awesome and she just tells me I'm fat and lazy." When I returned home, I remember her saying, "You've come back with a bit of an attitude and I'm not sure I like it."

I remember thinking that I could break it off with her, but instead I signed a year lease with her. I knew I should break up with her, but I was so scared. Where would I go? What would I do? Would I have to move in with my mom? When we finally broke up, I must have been ready, but I hadn't realized it. I probably could have broken up with her before I signed the lease. I look back at those ten months as "character building."

-Karen (Sydney)

Perhaps you want to resign due to stress. If you're leaving a very stressful job (say, air traffic controller or police officer) for a career you think will be less demanding (such as baker or office manager), you can probably be confident that the change in the nature of the job itself will result in less stress. But if you're leaving one job for something similar, such as an accountant moving from one firm to another, or from a firm to a private practice in hopes of reducing stress, how sure are you that your stress will be reduced? All accounting firms (like all work settings) have their own politics, pressures for performance from your bosses, nice people, jerks, and frustrating policies. Do you have concrete evidence that the new firm will provide a change of culture with less stress? What is that evidence?

Perhaps you're fed up with the politics of your job and want to start your own company. You can be confident that you will have fewer pressures for performance from your bosses, and fewer annoying coworkers and frustrating policies. You will likely, however, have increased stresses in the loneliness of running a solo business, self-imposed performance pressure, and logistics such as administration, paperwork and so on. It's important to examine the evidence for the reasons you're leaving so that you can determine what's in your control and what's not, and then identify the confidence you must make those things happen. Perhaps you are familiar with the challenges of running a business, and prefer solitary administration to your current work hassles, and so wouldn't be fazed by the practicalities of working solo. Perhaps your current job is so terrible, anything would be better. Or perhaps you investigate the challenges of solo practitioners and decide it's not for you. Whatever you choose, go into it with a clear head and with confidence.

Agung decided to stay at a critical point in his company's development. A previous decision to stay was based on wanting to know he'd done everything he could do to grow the company. Then he decided he was ready to move on.

I think I'm finished with this company. There's nothing more for me to fix, or learn, or gain or do. I squeezed that rock. I know for sure I did everything I could. The true test of being valued as a company is when your team can go on without you. It's nice when people feel like, "We can't live without you," but if you can't live without me, I haven't been a good leader. My priorities are different now, and I've made a plan to leave.

You can handle what comes your way

Many people who emigrated were not sure what they would find. They were confident, however, that whatever the challenges were, it would be better than staying where they were and that they would make it. Psychologists refer to this as having *self-efficacy*,[1] a belief in one's ability to succeed in specific situations or to accomplish a task. How does one develop self-efficacy? By doing the following:

- *Recognizing our own accomplishments.* First, it's important to recognize what we have been able to achieve to date, and to celebrate experiences where we attempted something difficult and were successful. Maybe we studied hard and learned French or became a good swimmer despite an aversion to water, or successfully got our child through the terrible twos. Even experiences of success unrelated to the current task at hand can help increase our belief in ourselves.
- *Observing someone else accomplishing the task.* Our choices are often affected by *observational learning*, or what we have seen others do. Seeking out successful role models is key — others who have trodden the path ahead and who have left home or their religion or their spouse and who are now happy and successful. Talk to them. Ask them for coffee, or set up an

informational interview. And what if you don't know anyone who has done what you're doing? How can I leave home and go to college when no one in my family ever has? Thankfully, there are many ways to address this. Even if no one in the family has gone to college, people outside the family have, which means it's possible. Find them and learn from what they've been through. This is called *learning from vicarious experience*. Physician Deborah German left her previous position to accept the role of Dean of the University of Central Florida's not-yet-existing college of medicine. When she was asked how she developed the confidence to start a medical school, she said, "Well, there are 140 medical schools in the U.S., each one of which was started by somebody. I told myself that if those 140 people could do it, so can I." So can you.

- *Setting appropriate boundaries.* It builds confidence to set boundaries and to be clear about what we will and will not accept. Sometimes when we feel we are being pushed around, or at times when we don't have any control, it's helpful to draw lines. This doesn't mean we can't change our minds later, as we go on figuring out what we really want. If we know that we will not miss one more of our child's baseball games because we are working late, then that is a good boundary to have. We might also set a boundary that this year has been a problem with missing ball games, but we will fix it for next year because it is not sustainable and not a way we want to live.

With my company, I'm setting boundaries about what I want and giving others the option to stay or leave me. My biggest customer is barbarian. This customer thinks they own me; they send incendiary emails. I really dislike working with them. I positioned my life to where I don't ever want to feel like I have to do that. ... When our contract comes up for renewal, I will tell them, "You have the choice to leave me or not, but the status quo is not an option. If you decide to stay, you will talk with us differently, work with us differently." That's part of the growth of my company. I've taken less work from this customer so I don't have to deal with their bullshit. I've already left them in my head. I don't need them.

-Agung (Connecticut)

- *Obtaining encouragement from others. Social persuasion* can be a useful tool to increase self-efficacy. Encouragement from others, especially from a mentor or someone who has been there, can increase confidence that you can do it. This doesn't mean you ask everyone to be a cheerleader for your every decision. It means asking selected people for their support as you decide what to do, and for constructive feedback, meaning they reflect on your actions and provide helpful suggestions (not insults or put-downs) to help you get to where you want to go, wherever that might be.

One of the best ways to learn build confidence is to hear from people who have been successful in making similar transitions. In the employment world, this is called "conducting informational interviews with people," but you can also just call it "asking questions." Thinking of changing jobs? Talk to someone in the job or field you're aiming to enter. Thinking of getting divorced? Talk with someone who has been divorced. Thinking of moving across the country? Ditto. Be sure to ask what they're happy about and what they're not happy about since leaving. What was difficult and what was easy. What they'd do differently if they had to do over again. Any one person will provide a useful perspective that is theirs, but it can be good to talk with three or four people or even more. See if the challenges they encountered are experiences you are confident that you too can overcome.

The big picture when I was considering leaving my abusive husband was my history. I left Cuba as a child. I was shuttled powerlessly from refugee camp to orphanage to foster homes until finally being reunited with my parents as a teenager. The only power I ever exercised was leaving my biological family at 18, Every other time I left somewhere it was because I was forced to. Then at 19, I fell into my husband's family, which was more dysfunctional than my family ever was. Years later, it took the help of a psychiatrist to extricate myself from him and his family. She helped me identify that I did have power, and how I could use that power to change my life.

-Linda (New York)

- *Changing your interpretation of your physiological state.* We feel more confident when we're relaxed, alert, generally happy, and expectant about the future. Too much anxiety can be crippling. Our interpretation of these physiological states can be important as well. If you feel your heart pound and your head spin, and you interpret that as anxiety or worse, that will not help you build confidence. Here's a secret: the physiological signs of anxiety can be nearly identical to the signs of excitement. Pounding heart? Sweating? Racing thoughts? Sounds like excitement to me! (Of course, if you have a medical condition, consult with your doctor.) When I feel those signs in myself, I do a quick body scan to ensure I'm okay, and then I make the deliberate choice to interpret those signs as excitement. I don't use the negative self-talk of, "Wow, I'm anxious. This is a big deal. I hope I get it right!" Instead, I say to myself, "Wow! I am so excited about this. It's going to be great!" Does that mean everything in my life is always roses? Of course not. But I do find I feel a lot better, regardless of what happens, if I go into it with a feeling of anticipatory excitement instead of with anxiety or worry.

Taking chances will be worth it

Confidence includes the belief that even if things don't work out exactly as you hoped, it was still worth it. This requires having a broad view of what life is about, a sense of humor about yourself, and faith that your life is unfolding exactly as it should.

I visited a general practitioner in India whose words have stuck with me. He brought his holistic health beliefs into his practice, and after asking me about my interest in medicine and mental health, he didn't pause for a moment but said, "It is inevitable." I looked back at him, confused, and he continued, "It is inevitable that we would meet, that we would have this conversation. It is inevitable that I learn from you about mental health, and that you will hopefully learn something from me – I don't know what you will learn, but it is inevitable that this would happen. This is a step you must take into your destiny." He of course didn't know it, but he was planting the seeds that were indeed part of my destiny. His insistence on inevitability made me ask myself about what I think is inevitable in my life. Not just death and taxes, but what is my true destiny? What is it I am here to accomplish? What is it that is inevitable and must happen?

Be gentle with yourself. You are a child of the universe no less than the trees and the stars; you have a right to be here.

And whether or not it is clear to you, no doubt the universe is unfolding as it should.

-Poet Max Erhmann[2]

Author Susan Jeffers[3] talks about positive affirmations, by telling herself that whatever happens in her life, she will learn and grow from it. She insists on finding a way to make whatever happens in her life an enriching experience. She also likes to repeat, "It's all happening perfectly."

Repeat this as many times as it takes.

You don't have to leap all at once, but developing this confidence can help you take the steps to explore what you want to do at a comfortable pace.

Forcing yourself to take little chances can have unexpected benefits. Catherine Morrison, a fantastic negotiation and conflict management consultant based in Portland, Maine, talks about improving your skills through little everyday negotiations just to practice – for example, requesting an upgrade at a hotel, or a better table at a restaurant. It's essentially being more aware of what we want and how we might ask for it. Over time, we will increase our confidence about what we want, and can soon learn how to take the steps to ask for it.

Muri hadn't seriously considered leaving Nigeria, but put his name in the U.S. visa lottery as a joke. He turned away phone calls twice before realizing he had actually won the lottery. He now lives in New Orleans with his wife and two children.

I was working in oil and gas in Nigeria and hadn't really thought of leaving. When I realized the visa was real, I knew it was a once in a lifetime opportunity. So I took a very big leap – I left Nigeria by myself, and left my wife and infant son behind. Within a few years, I brought my wife and son to the U.S., and now we have another son. The opportunity here in the U.S. is so incredible, and I'm so glad I took the leap.

-Muri (New Orleans and Nigeria)

I once bought a house with someone I had been dating for nine months. I remember thinking at the time that it was a pretty crazy move, but I felt drawn toward it. I thought about it over and over, and finally decided, "This is what I have to do. I'm not sure why, but I'm going to do it. Maybe the lesson to learn is 'Don't move in with someone after nine months,' but I just feel I have to do this." And I'm very glad I did. We had a good relationship and had so much fun in that house. Although neither the relationship nor the house is still in my life, I'm so glad I took that leap. And it helped increase my confidence to take more chances.

Taking chances can pay off in a big way. Here's another example. I had a job that started off very well but became a bad fit, I and wasn't feeling very confident about the next steps. When I went to a national conference, I made a deal with myself that I would say to just one person, "I am just starting to think about what else might be out there." In retrospect, it's not a very strong statement, but it was very difficult to make myself say it. Toward the end of the conference, someone asked me how it was going, and I recited my sentence, "I am just starting to think about what else might be out there." There was a pause and she said kindly, "Tell me what you are looking for." I stumbled through a response that I wasn't really looking and wasn't even sure that I wanted to leave, but that I was open to a place that was larger and more diverse. After another pause, she said, "You should contact so-and-so. Tell her I sent you. She just moved to a new place and is looking for new colleagues." I did contact so-and-so, after an embarrassing week of delays due to my own self-doubt. Our conversation went well, and not long after, so-and-so offered me a position. What a great confidence-booster for putting myself out there!

Challenges to increasing your confidence

Sometimes people are offended or upset by your growth. This doesn't mean it's wrong to grow. For example, some parents love being parents of little kids. They love being *needed*. I'm sure you can see where this is going. Kids are supposed to grow up and become more independent, but if a parent is really invested in being needed, how is that going to work long-term for the child? If the parents don't tolerate the child's growth, or if they directly or indirectly indicate that he or she should be dependent on them that will interfere with the child's normal growth and development. Often people who are like this try to make their problem *your* problem. As in a parent telling the child (not necessarily in words), "When you grow, it makes me upset and insecure about who I am and my role in your life, so you should stop growing and stop becoming independent." This happens frequently in professional settings as well. I've seen it repeatedly where senior colleagues are very interested and enthusiastic about helping students or early career professionals. Once the junior colleagues start achieving, however, the senior colleague starts seeing them as competition and withdraws support. The senior colleague may even start undermining the junior colleague. In reality, other people's problems are *not* your problem.

Another challenge is that your loved ones may not like your new direction and may sabotage you unintentionally or intentionally. For example, when one person decides to quit smoking, or exercise, or eat healthier, sometimes other family members feel threatened or judged. In some situations, they may actively undermine the person who's seeking to improve their health by smoking around them, offering alcohol, or buying junk food.

Even before you make any decisions about leaving, increasing your confidence is, in my view, a very good strategy. Increase your confidence in your ability to persevere and to handle what life throws at you. Try some of the ideas above and watch your self-belief increase. If you're struggling, note this: Every single person I listened to about leaving said they did not regret leaving. Most said, in fact, that their only regret was not leaving sooner. How's that for confidence-building?

Chapter 6: Decision

My solo three-month hike on the Pacific Crest Trail had many beginnings. There was the first, flip decision to do it, followed by the second, more serious decision to actually do it, and then the long third beginning, composed of weeks of shopping and packing and preparing to do it. ... At long last, there was the actual doing it, quickly followed by the grim realization of what it meant to do it, followed by the decision to quit doing it because doing it was absurd and pointless and ridiculously difficult and far more than I expected doing it would be and I was profoundly unprepared to do it. And then there was the real live truly doing it.

—Cheryl Strayed, *Wild*[1]

At this point, let's say you have experienced that glimmer of light – the possibility that something can be different. You've probably gone back and forth, telling yourself, "No, I couldn't possibly do that," and then "Well, maybe..." and then back to "Impossible!" You've begun to solidify the hope that things truly could be better. Not a guarantee, but the hope is growing that a change will be better than no change. Great! Next, you worked on your confidence that you could navigate the change associated with the leaving you're considering. You looked at possibilities of "What if I ..." You identified examples where you have successfully made significant change or where others have made similar changes. You've increased your confidence to where you're thinking that you could really do this. So now the next step is... Should you leave?

There's nothing wrong with cutting out at this point. You can decide that it was interesting to think about leaving, but that it's not for you. That's fine. As we've said, leaving can be scary, or ill-timed. But you've come this far, so let's walk through considerations for your actual decision. A word of warning. Like Cheryl Strayed, your "decision" may be a series of decisions, indecision, and changing your mind over a long period of time. When you have the luxury of time, give yourself the space to slow down the process and think through what you want.

Making the right decision

We'll come back to this in Chapter 9, *Integration*, but for now, let's try another game. I'd like you to consider the option of removing the angst over, "Will I make the right decision?" Think of your decision as a puzzle, or a brain teaser. Given x information about my current situation, y information about the possibility of leaving and what that might lead to, and z goals that I have for my life, what is the best decision to make? Super fun, right? Of course it's not just a rational, logical decision, but what if we pretended it was?

For example:

x – *information about my current situation:* Job only pays $27,000 annually.

y – *information about the possibility of leaving:* I have a good chance of a job paying $34,000 annually, but it would mean moving to another area and the related upheaval and expense.

z – *my life goals*: Long term, I'd like to live away from my family and experience a new location. The new job will also advance me in my chosen career.

Conclusion: I'm going to go for it!

One of my favorite tools is making lists. Creating such a list is a fascinating exercise to help you understand more about what making a decision means to you. Here are some lists you can make, to get your brain moving and to reduce anxiety.

State your goals. What kind of life do you want to live? Note this exercise is harder than it looks. What will be in your life that will make you think, "Aaaah, I'm *so* happy!" Think about:

- Where you might live
- Who would be in your life
- What would you do with your time
- What impact you would have on people
- What would be your legacy
- What kinds of experiences you would have
- What a typical day might look like

Don't hold back on this. And don't go for the silly "mansion, jet skis, champagne" lifestyle choices without pushing yourself harder to dig deeper. You may feel the anxiety of, "This is impossible" creeping in, but leave that for later. Author Tim Ferriss talks about how our wildest dreams may be even easier than we think, which we can find out when we calculate the actual costs of a trip to Paris or a fancy car.[2] Don't get stuck in that wistfulness and longing of, "If only I went to Paris, or looked up that former girlfriend, or bought the car I want."

People regret the things they didn't do, not the things they did. So do it. Figure out what you really want your life to be.

True courage comes from doing something and not knowing the outcome. That's where hope comes in. I knew things at work wouldn't get better. I had to look at my own life. I want to be good to my customers, but that doesn't come at the cost of my dignity. And that's why I'm leaving my company.

-Agung (Connecticut)

I have certain food connections that I firmly believe (despite all implausibility) help me think. Junior Mints help me complete a research proposal. Middle Eastern food (hummus, rolled grape leaves, tabbouli) helps me focus, and mojitos help me think big. I know it doesn't make sense, but it works for me! The last few significant decisions, I found that mojitos assisted me in letting go of the inhibitions in dreaming big. For example, I sat on a beach, mesmerized by the gentle waves, and while sipping mojitos, dreamed much bigger than usual.

So often we think, "What if I fail?" or, "What's the worst that could happen?" But I really wanted to think about, "What if I am wildly successful?" Mojitos let me really consider, "If I knew I wouldn't fail, what would I want to do with the next few years of my life?" It gave me the space and the courage to leave some situations that weren't working for me, to start planning this book, and to conceptualize a totally different life for myself. I wouldn't call this a "new" life, but rather a continuation of my current life trajectory, and it has been enormously satisfying.

Ricci is planning to leave New York City, where he has lived for the past 17 years. He lives in Manhattan, but not too far from his parents. In his culture, parents are very protective and children stay close to home. He is interested in making a new start on his own in another city, perhaps London, Amsterdam, or Barcelona. He wants the enjoyment of, "Starting from zero, finding an apartment, having to furnish it, and finding new friends." His fantasy is to move to Barcelona, work as a waiter, read, and work on his Spanish. He said that in his fantasy, it will be like "three months of therapy." His only fears are that when he gets to the new place, he will feel the same as he does now, or even worse.

I'm not in any way suggesting that mojitos are the only key to smart decision making. I am suggesting, however, that it may be useful to put yourself in a space, through mojitos or yoga or running, or whatever works for you that allows you to reach beyond your current life to consider what else is *possible*. Because that's what's really exciting, right? Not just what is, but what is possible.

Don't forget to breathe. It's okay if your goals overwhelm you a little. In fact, if your goals don't overwhelm you, you might not be aiming high enough. Remember, this is your *life*.

Clearly define the options on the table right now. Once you're clear on your goals, it's time to clearly define the options. At this step, I'm reminded of when I worked with elementary schoolchildren, and I would often help them problem solve. I would ask a child, for example, "What are some things you could do if someone pushes you in line?" The child would usually look sheepish and say something civil like, "Tell the teacher," or "Ask them to stop." Usually I would have to point out that they *could* hit the other kid. When I would say this, their eyes would get really big and they would say, "No," (even if they were sent to me specifically because they were hitting people who accidentally pushed them in line). Learning what *all* of the options are can help us improve in our ability to assess possibilities and determine what works for us and what doesn't.

Your options may be as simple as, "Stay with my boyfriend" versus, "Break up with my boyfriend." But it could also be, "Stay with my boyfriend" versus, "Dump all his things on the front lawn," or, "Break up with my boyfriend because I'm really still in love with my ex," or, "Sell everything I own and sail solo around the world." (The latter is my go-to fantasy escape.)

How you frame your options is important. Don't second guess yourself here or limit yourself. Think of *all* the possibilities, even if they might seem silly. It's okay if you get overwhelmed and need to stop for a while.

Have a mojito if you need to (or a run) and then get back to it when you're ready. Often I find that when we do this exercise, we often find other areas of our lives that we want to change as well. It may end up being not just about the boyfriend. It may be the boyfriend, the job, the apartment, the city, and the whole life that needs some attention. Maybe the boyfriend is the loose piece of yarn that unravels the whole sweater. That's okay. And again, it's okay to be overwhelmed. Think about what you want from your life. You don't have to do it all at once, and you don't even have to do any of it. But do give yourself the space to dream about what you want.

Think about your contingencies. What are the considerations that you need to take into account when you consider leaving? Here are some examples:

- Children or other family members
- Finances
- Culture
- Religion
- Health issues
- Fear

The trick with this step is to keep anxiety and worry in check. Just one step at a time here. Any contingencies you identify do not negate everything you've done so far. Don't let yourself go down a rabbit hole of practicalities and logistics, such as, "I don't have a lot of money, so I can never leave home, and I should stop thinking about it now." Hang in there and list the things you will need to consider. Just make the list.

Ask some more challenging questions. Now comes the really interesting part. Remember this is just a thought experiment at this point. You are not compelled to *do* anything. It's just thinking about what you want. For many of us, thinking about our goals and what we want is a double mind-whammy. Now it's time to dig more deeply into the details. Anxiety might ratchet up; that's okay. Take a break, do some deep breathing, and keep going.

- What am I trying to get out of leaving? (Note, "just something different" is a totally acceptable answer, but push yourself to think beyond that and to be more specific.)
- What would happen if I stay?
- How is this decision consistent or inconsistent with my goals?
- What will I leave behind? What will I go toward?
- What will I learn from this experience?
- Am I concerned about what people will think of me? How much does this matter?
- In what ways can this go wrong? (You probably have a lot of examples of this.)
- In what ways can this go very right? (Push yourself on this one.)

Make a pros and cons list

A pros and cons list is a beautiful thing. I like to divide a piece of paper into four quadrants (folding works nicely). The top two quadrants can be the pros and cons of staying, and the bottom two of leaving. Start filling them in. You can keep the list to yourself if you want, unless you decide to share. You may find, as I do, that the list starts to feel silly because you can't possibly put into words all that you're feeling. That's okay. Try anyway. As above, you will need to clarify exactly what you mean by "leaving" and "staying." Great! That's the idea. Once you have your lists on the paper, you may already have made your decision. Or, you could decide that what you really need is to get more information on particular issues. That's also a good outcome. I have found in my use of a pros/cons list, I always learn something. Sometimes I decide to stay, sometimes I decide to leave, but it always helps me clarify what I'm thinking and what I need to get more information on.

Trust your intuition

Maybe you haven't been much in touch with that voice in your head that guides you when you need it. But intuition can be so valuable, above and beyond all of the rational and logical tables and charts (which were just to get you thinking anyway). Intuition kicks in when you *know* what the right thing to do is because you feel it in your soul and in your bones.

For example, when I lived in Portland, Oregon, every day I would walk my dog by a house in my neighborhood. It was a beautiful green house on a small hill with a big front porch and a beautiful style. The first time I walked by, I thought, "I'm going to live in that house." This was just preposterous, because I was very happy with where I was living, literally two blocks away. I don't even know where the thought came from. Five years later, I was looking for a house with my new partner. We had looked nearly everywhere, when I finally thought of the green house. I walked by again and there was a very small sign saying that it was for sale. I looked in the windows and it was empty. Again, that voice in my head said, "I'm going to live in this house." And of course it happened. This has occurred several times in my life, and my intuition has always led me in the right direction.

Ways to get in touch with your intuition: meditate, be open to whatever the universe brings, create an intention, and follow your inner leading.

Decide the best option (or sometimes the least bad option).
Even if you do all the preparation suggested in this chapter, the actual decision could still be where you get stuck. It may be that you're simply not ready to decide. Ask yourself if you need to make the decision now or if it could wait. Can you set it to one side while you mull things over, consciously or unconsciously? Identify your sticking points (these may be similar what we tell ourselves to extinguish the glimmer of light of change, described in Chapter 4, *Awareness*). If you have time, keep working through these steps and decide when you need to. Sometimes, you need to sleep on it and allow yourself time for decisions to surface. If time is short, push yourself to think, let go, meditate, go running, have a mojito, or discuss it with a trusted friend or counselor.

A lesson I heard as a child in Sunday School was that God gave one of three answers to prayers: Yes, No, or Wait. This was baffling to me then, but now I see that it's rooted in wisdom. As you think about your options, clarify whether each one could be a yes, a no, or a wait. What is compelling you to make a decision right now? What are the risks of waiting?

Know that you will make the right decision
There is no certainty about what will happen next, and how things will turn out. There is only the knowledge that we made the best decision we could, given the information we had at the time. We have so many decisions to make, including what to have for breakfast, and what to wear today. This big decision we are considering now is one that requires thought and consideration, and it also requires *making a decision*. Not making a decision is a decision in itself as well. I think it's better actively to make decisions instead of passively letting life decide for us. Trust that what you decided is right for you.

I was working as a travel journalist and on a cruise ship when I met a man. He heard me talking in Swedish to my photographer and asked if I was Swedish. His grandparents are from Sweden. I met him on Valentine's Day under a full moon. I'm not that romantic, but even so, it was too much! We spent four days together on the ship. I visited him in the U.S. twice, and after a grand total of 14 days together, I left Sweden and my family and my home there to move in with him in the U.S. It's been 11 years, and not once did I feel like I made the wrong decision.

-Petra (Sweden)

Simple, right? As many of us know, making a decision is not always this straightforward. There are few people who can go from confidence to decision in a single afternoon. We have different comfort points for deciding. Some of us have a default for "stay," and it would take a whole lot to get us to leave. Others of us have a default to "leave," and once we get that itch to move on, it becomes harder and harder to stay. I talked to many leavers who said that once they get it in their head that they need to leave a job or apartment, they just can't fully rest until they figure it out and leave. But as stated, it's important to give ourselves time to think through our options.

Make a decision and then make the decision right. Line up your energy with it. In most cases, it doesn't really matter what you decide. Just decide. There are endless options that would serve you enormously well, and all or any one of them is better than no decision.

-Spiritualist Esther Hicks[3]

Whatever your default is, finding a way to identify your reasons, your evidence, and your emotions can help make a more informed decision. It's not likely to be easy to leave, but if the decision is made in a thoughtful, sensitive way, you can be assured it was right – or good enough, or the best you could do at the time. Trust that there will be the space and opportunity to adjust things afterwards and to tie up any loose ends. Decisions are not always static and final.

Now the kids are almost gone and I'm not sure if I could leave where I live. I am an adventurer. I don't like to stay home. I'm physically trying to move out of my house. Still, the thought of moving is so overwhelming, so each week, I do something to upgrade or purge stuff. Maybe I am able to do all of my adventuring because I have my home as a sanctuary.

-Liz (Connecticut)

In the end, it's not always a logical decision. In many cases, it's a gut decision. It becomes clear. The point is not to ensure you make the most logical decision, it's to ensure you make the decision that's right for you. Doing these exercises provides tools to think through the factors involved, and to help move you towards clarity.

Yes, I'm leaving
What leads people to decide that yes, now is the time to leave?

- Emily in Oregon, a self-confessed stayer, decided to move across the U.S. to take a job at a federal agency. She said, "As much as I loved my job here on the west coast, this was a once in a lifetime opportunity. *I knew I'd kick myself if I didn't take it.*"
- After a lull in work, Geoff from Canada decided to take a road trip through the western U.S. He said, "*There's more reason to go than to stay put.* There's more out there once you get moving and you're actually living life."
- Christine from Connecticut said, "My husband and I separated because we have different lifestyles. He's overweight, he drinks and takes drugs, and he parties a lot. I'm focused on being healthy. I thought we could make it work, but after nine years, *I couldn't take it anymore.*"
- Clark from New York said, "Leaving my marriage was years in the making and it happened in a split second. My wife was emotionally abusive and financially controlling, but her controlling had convinced me everything was my fault. My best friend saw how bad things were and she said, 'You need to leave.' I said I would think about making a plan and she

said, 'Screw the plan. You can move out this weekend. I'll help you.' I went from years of thinking, 'This is all in my head and I'm doing this wrong' to suddenly someone else validating everything. Years of thinking, 'I want to leave but can't leave,' suddenly turned into '*DO IT NOW*.'"

- Eric from New York said, "*I had turned into a person I couldn't recognize.* I'm not the type of person to yell at my boss, yell at the company president. Ultimately, I didn't like them. I was so frustrated. I think the breaking point came when a good friend who was also a mentor passed away giving birth. Toward the end, that sent me the message I need to change."

- Martin and his partner Javier decided to move to Peru after Javier discovered a heart condition that meant he would have trouble getting insurance in the U.S. "*We decided it was time,*" Martin said. "There's a sense of solitude and peacefulness in Peru that I don't feel in the U.S."

- Kim from Connecticut said she doesn't like to be left behind, so she stayed with an abusive, alcoholic husband for 16 years until she reached a point where she wanted to leave. "*I had to reach a point where I couldn't stand being with him so that I could leave.* I should have left after the first year."

No, I'm staying

What kinds of insights make people decide to stay?

- Billy from Louisiana described how he made a choice to stay. He and his partner, Robert, were arguing. "We were having a big argument and were on the brink of splitting up. I decided that if I left, I'd have to go through all this stuff with another person and go through the same thing I'm going through now. I thought to myself, 'Instead of going through all that again, *I'm going to clean this mess up now*.' I've been a stayer ever since."

- Agung from Connecticut said he stayed in his job because he felt like he wasn't done yet. "I *stay if there's hope and if I feel like I've done everything I can* to make things better."

- Katrina from New York said, "*This is where I want to be.* This is where I can truly be myself."

- Nikkia from Atlanta moved several times for work and for adventure. She stopped moving when she had children. "Having children didn't change me, and I still get restless. I just feel a *responsibility toward my family* to stay put."

And on the "I'll wait" side:

- Alma from Washington DC said, "I'm staying in this job at least until my son graduates from high school. Then I'll have more options. Until then, I'm learning as much as I can."
- Hugo from Colombia said, "I'm not sure if I want to move back to Colombia or stay in the U.S. Right now, I'm going to wait and see what happens."
- George in New York is a faculty member at a large university. He told me his boss made racist comments to him, and his work was being judged unfairly because he complained about the racism. He was concerned that if he leaves in the middle of the academic year, he won't be able to find another job. So he's staying put until he figures out his next step.

Go. Stop thinking and just pack your shit, buy a plane ticket, or pack your car and just go. Everything will fall into place. Everything's always okay in the end.

-Geoff (Vancouver)

When I first started leaving, I was insecure about next steps. I felt as if I were swinging from branch to branch, wanting to be sure I had the next branch firmly in hand before I let go of the last one. People still said I was brave — I didn't believe them, as I didn't feel brave because I felt I was still holding on and not truly making the leap.

Some circumstances are more challenging to let go of without knowing your next step. Many if not most people want to have a new job in hand before they leave the old one. This could be a matter of logistics. Most people get divorced or break up without a new girlfriend or boyfriend, but some people need to know they won't be alone before they can take the plunge. Sometimes it's the new opportunity (new job or new prospective spouse) that helps us make up our minds that the previous option is no longer tenable. Many times, however, we need to make a leap and trust that the net will appear.

I tried leaving my abusive ex-husband three times. My lawyer was afraid of my ex's family. The first time I went to him, my lawyer said, "You're crying too hard. You don't want to get a divorce." The second time I went to the lawyer, I started crying again. The lawyer said, "You're still too emotional. You're not ready." The third time, I came in angry and said, "I want a divorce now." The lawyer said, "Okay!"

-Kim (Connecticut)

Making the leap feels a little scary, of course, but you also have to think, "What's the worst that could happen?" and "What's the best that could happen?" A fall doesn't have to be catastrophic, and even awful scenarios (such as, "I'm alone forever," or, "I'll go bankrupt") are highly unlikely, no matter how much our minds may seize on them. And we often can't imagine how delightful our future can be. By following this thoughtful process, you're more likely to make a decision from a position of strength and evidence, rather than out of fear and anxiety.

There are many rational arguments for leaving. You're not being paid enough money, you have a poor relationship with your boss, your relationship just doesn't have the same spark anymore. Maybe you have more ambition than your partner, or much less. Maybe you have differences of opinion. There are plenty of reasons. But ultimately it comes down to knowing that you must go, you must move on. Or, perhaps, despite the unease you feel, knowing that you need to stay, at least for now. Recognizing that feeling in yourself is so incredibly important. Being able to take it apart, examine it, look at it without panicking and hyperventilating, and to see what it is while taking deep breaths – all this is key. Know in your bones that the process is important, not just the outcome.

Chapter 7: Preparation

Congratulations! You've made your decision. It's time to work out how and when to move forward! Preparing to leave, when you're serious about leaving, takes every bit of fortitude that you have. Or maybe by the time you're leaving, your fortitude is steel. Now's the time to set any fear and trepidation aside. You can start looking at timing, logistics and everything else associated with leaving.

I consider the main issues to address are *logistics*, *feelings*, and *courage*. Part of the challenge of moving on is when all these things feel jumbled up in our heads and lead to anxiety, which can lead to us rethinking our decision to leave. It's fine to reconsider the decision (see the previous chapter), but I suggest doing that from a place of strength and calm, not a place of anxiety and fear. Let's jump in!

This chapter discusses how to prepare to leave any kind of situation. It's important to note that some areas are easier to tackle, and others much more difficult. Some people struggle most with the logistics; others are more uncomfortable with the emotional aspects of leaving or with communicating. Take your time and think carefully about each of these sections before you proceed. Note which areas are easier or harder for you, seek support, and be easy on yourself. Sometimes, of course, you don't have the luxury of time. Clark from New York was offered a job the Wednesday before Labor Day – on condition that he start the Tuesday after the holiday weekend. He hustled and got it done. As Stephen from Washington DC said, "If you don't have time, you just have to learn to think faster – and quickly!"

Logistics
I am fantastic at catastrophic thinking, in which I can come up with every possible thing that could go wrong, regardless of how implausible. I have worked hard over the years to turn that questionable skill into a strength. I think I have successfully relabeled

it: rather than catastrophic thinking, it's a skill of risk assessment! A realistic appraisal of any hazards, plus my years of hands-on experience in packing up and going, mean that I am now excellent at logistics! So, drawn from my extensive experience, this section covers all the things that need to be done before you leave.

Logistics are the foundation of any move. They can include items to bring, training in self-defense, financial management and other activities. Plenty of online resources outline logistical activities to prepare for transitions. For example, there are websites on, "How to prepare for the trip of a lifetime," which list what to pack when leaving for an adventure. Or, "Ten things to do before you leave your job" identifies steps such as arranging for transfer of health insurance, disability insurance, or retirement accounts, as well as having a financial cushion if there is a break between jobs.

The Runaway's Diary[1] by Marilyn Harris is subtitled, "The story of a girl on a journey in search of herself." The title character, 15-year-old Cat, runs away from home to hitchhike to the Catskills and make a life for herself. In her diary, which begins just before she runs away, Cat details things to take, including a tent, blanket, flashlight, clean shirt, sweater, pants, and diary. She debates whether to take a towel and decides it's too much, and pins money to the inside of her pants. When she leaves, she is confident in her preparations.

When I plan to leave, I start a notebook with lists of what I need to do. This helps me keep the logistics tasks out of my head, so that I have space to feel without being bogged down by details. I carry the notebook around and write notes whenever something new occurs to me. (Some people may prefer to use their phone for this purpose.) A great place to start with logistics is asking the question, "What worries me most?" Then start writing out what can be done about that.

For example, suppose you are leaving for adventure. Sounds glamorous, but many would-be adventurers get stuck on planning. You don't have to fling yourself into the unknown with no preparation just because you're an adventurer, although some people do! How much planning you do, and how enjoyable or stressful it is, really has to do with your own sense of yourself and your preferences. John Steinbeck and Cheryl Strayed planned in great detail, spent time carefully considering what to bring and where to go, and reflected that the planning time was worth it. But William Finnegan grabbed his surf gear and hit the road, traveling from one surf spot to the next. He also spent at least a week eating only canned beans and fish he caught on a deserted beach when he had run out of supplies. It really depends on your comfort level.

So, first, it makes sense for new adventurers to think about their adventure comfort zone. No judgment: just what you like and don't like. Here are a few questions to get you started:
- Do you prefer to know every day where you're staying that night, or are you comfortable figuring it out as you go? For my adventures I often reserve first and last nights' lodging, and then improvise for everything in between.
- How anxious do you get when you can't immediately find food, hotel, shelter, etc.?
- How comfortable are you being surrounded by people who don't speak your language? When you have to express what you need to others who don't speak your language, is that fun or extremely stressful? (I am always surprised when others ask, "How did you manage when you don't speak the language?" It's easier than you think!)
- How well do you tolerate insects, heat, cold, dirt, and discomfort? Do you get extremely anxious if you can't shower every day? Do

you have health issues such as allergies or asthma that may be very real considerations? (Not limitations, just considerations.)

- How much alone time do you need? (hostel vs. hotel) How much can you tune out chaos around you vs. getting bothered by it?
- Do you prefer fancy food or street food or in between?
- When you travel somewhere, do you read up on everything to do in the area and have a checklist of must-see sites, or have a general idea and figure it out when you get there?
- What is your budget, and in what areas do you want to splurge or be frugal?

Once you've identified your comfort zone, you can decide how much you want to push the boundaries — a little, or a lot. I suggest that if you're not used to adventures or if you have a relatively narrow comfort zone, build up gradually to a larger adventure. Start with a day trip a few hours away from where you live. Plan one thing to do or see and drive there or take the bus or train. When you go, pay attention to what you do and how you feel. Does the bus feel uncomfortably crowded? How much do you investigate your destination in advance – do you find out its opening hours and history and read up on it, or just go and figure it out when you're there? What about when you get hungry? Or when things don't go exactly as planned? How comfortable are you interacting with other people?

Once you have a little adventuring experience under your belt, you can work on planning something larger, while adjusting for your comfort zone. Maybe, for example, you'll eat anything but are very particular about where you sleep, and need cleanliness, darkness, and quiet. In that case, reserve a great hotel and be adventurous with eating and daytime activities.

Now we've considered your comfort zone, let's start looking at the logistics.

If you're leaving for adventure, then, here's a partial list of what might go on your preparations book:

- Flight/boat/car itinerary/guidebook
- Money and credit cards
- Clothes/inclement weather gear
- Phone and chargers
- Passport and visas
- Writing materials/cards/stamps

- Toiletries
- Emergency contacts
- Plan for self-care, including taking time to rest, physically caring for yourself, and obtaining emotional support from friend

This is just to get you started – there are many useful web pages with more detail which you can use to customize your particular trip needs. You may find it useful to think about your comfort zone in relation to other life changes, too, and to use the same principle of dipping a toe in the water before taking the final step. For example, you could spend a weekend or longer vacation in the place where you want to move, or spend more time alone or with friends before deciding to split up with a partner. While an adventure can be more open-ended, it also tends to be short term and may not have long-lasting implications (although some people's lives have been changed on adventures!) Other life changes such as a house move or divorce are more defined and limited and have more complicated logistics and long-term effects. So let's look at the logistical concerns of other areas now.

If you're moving away, you may be worried about finding a new apartment or house, packing up your belongings, renting a truck, driving to the new place. In this case, I would make a list of all these things.

Here is a partial to-do list:

- What I'm looking for in a new place to live and leads on possible new homes
- Packing supplies needed
- Belongings to sell / discard
- What to pack
- Timeline for packing
- Contents of last-out, first-in box (sheets, toiletries, valuables)
- Plan for trash removal
- Moving day details (truck rental, moving estimates, who will help you move)
- What to do when you arrive at the new place
- Utilities to start or stop
- Address change materials to submit
- Financial accounting
- Whatever else is worrying you
- Plan for self-care, including taking time to rest, physically caring for yourself, and obtaining emotional support from friends

---

When I moved to Dayton, Ohio, I drove a truck with my stuff and towed my car. After about two hours of driving, in the middle of nowhere, right front wheel bearings popped out and scattered all over the shoulder, and my moving adventure and ground to a halt. A farmer let me use his phone to call the truck rental company, and he let my cat and me stay warm while we waited. They towed the truck the rest of the way.

-Gerry (Ohio)

If you are considering leaving a job, here is a partial to-do list:

- Preparing your team for the transition (begin transferring projects) possibly before you tell them you are leaving
- Tell staff including administrative staff and colleagues (create a plan; prepare for reactions; letters)
- Transfer of responsibilities/meetings
- Finish projects
- Move belongings (home/office)
- Goodbye parties/lunches
- Create plan for starting at new job (first 100 days)
- Change of address for professional contacts
- Business cards / announcements at new place
- Start meeting people (listen and build relationships; lunch)
- Start implementing plan for leaving
- Remember your story and opportunity to start fresh
- Send note back to former employer / colleagues to maintain relationship
- Plan for self-care, including taking time to rest, physically caring for yourself, and obtaining emotional support from friends

If you're leaving a partner, here's a partial list of what you might need to consider:

- Safety of yourself, children, and pets
- Securing finances like bank accounts, retirement, life insurance
- Identifying where to live
- Transferring assets like car or properties
- Dividing belongings
- Divorce/separation paperwork
- Plan to secure important documents (birth

- certificates, Social Security)
- How to tell children, close friends, relatives about the separation
- Update emergency contacts

- Plan for self-care, including taking time off, physically caring for yourself, and obtaining emotional support from friends

My ex-husband and I used to joke that we could never get divorced, because we had too much stuff. When we divorced, however, separating our belongings was a piece of cake. He took the (newly purchased) house, I took the (reliable) car. I got the dishes; he got the silverware. The hardest thing to divide was (dating myself here) the music CDs. We each took back our own, and then we horse-traded: he took Bob Marley in exchange for my picking the Neville Brothers. Or was it vice versa? Maybe I specifically didn't want the Neville Brothers, because we fell in love listening to some of their songs. Trading CDs was like replaying the soundtrack to our relationship.

One final note about logistics. I love logistics. I am very good at logistics. And sometimes I focus on logistics because I don't want to feel the emotional part. It's easier for me to coordinate supplies, packing, moving van, utilities turn-off, new utilities turn-on, cleaning, unpacking, and trash removal, than it is to truly let myself feel the loss of the neighbors I loved, the corner store staff who were always so kind, the joy I felt when I moved into this home. These emotional needs are too important to be overshadowed by logistics. Let's consider these now.

Emotional needs

We may want to work on mental strategies to shore up our resolve to begin the transition. In *The Runaway's Diary*, Cat makes a list about things she'll miss, including her dog and her bedroom, sets out a list of rules for herself ("I shall not complain if I am ever cold or hot or hungry or dirty"; "I shall be a friend to everyone I meet"), and documents her reasoning for running away. Such documentation may

112

be especially useful in the early stages of leaving to remind ourselves of why we are going. Another mental strategy is to imagine the future and to give ourselves a pep talk about the adventures to come, even when we're not sure what they will be. Here are some items you may want to write about to address your emotional needs:

- Reasons for leaving
- Concerns/worries (but don't go overboard here)
- Things you enjoyed about the situation you're leaving or special moments you don't want to forget
- Plans for how you will move forward in describing the leaving
- How you anticipate your life will be different after you leave
- A pep talk to yourself
- Preparations for how you want the transition moment to go
- A list of friendly, supportive people to call that you know will be on your side and are available when you feel stuck, sad, or unhappy

Each of these items will not alone resolve all your emotional needs around the transition. They can, however, assist you in paying attention to the emotional work associated with leaving. It may make sense to spend a little time working in your leaving book each night, or to carry it around with you to write in when you start to feel anxious or worried.

There shouldn't be any shame or stigma in leaving. There shouldn't be any fear of the unknown. It's only when you walk away from something that you can actually walk towards something else, even if you don't know what that something else is.

-Anita (Nairobi)

Identify your story about leaving and use it as a mantra

I mentioned that when I was in difficult leaving situations, I often made time to write out why I was leaving. I started this process because I was anxious I might regret it, so I wanted to keep for posterity my reasons for leaving based on the currently available information. Although in some instances, I look back and found that some of my assumptions were wrong, or I occasionally found out information that could have influenced me, I am proud of my reasoning and my choices.

Writing down our reasoning can be helpful in coming up with our story. This is not a suggestion to create a falsehood or to try to deceive anyone, but rather a story that is true and clear and which feels good with who you are – and which also can be a default statement when you're feeling a bit shaky or upset. The key thing is that your story fits you.

Karen left Sydney for London, returned to Sydney, returned to London, and left London for the U.S. She has also left home, partners, jobs, and her family.

When I left for London the first time, people kept asking me why. When people ask me, "Why are you leaving?" my answer is always, "Why not?" That is seriously the only answer everyone always gets out of me. I used to say, 'Life is short, you should live it, et cetera," but I don't even say that anymore. My sister [who passed away] taught me to take life by the horns because she didn't. She was always saving for a big rainy day. That's not what life is about for me. I think people should experience life and live it, even if their version of really living is walking to the corner store or sitting in front of the TV and playing video games. Just do it. A friend in London will say, "Hey Karen, do you want to…?" and she doesn't even finish the sentence and I say yes. My answer is always, "Why not?" I can't find a reason why not.

-Karen (Sydney)

Sometimes the story is easy to come up with: "I'm leaving this job to go to school." "Our friendship faded because I moved away." Sometimes, though, it takes a little more nuance. I left a job once where there was a lot of negativity and mixed messages; it had become a bad fit. When people asked why I was leaving, I wanted to tell them in detail what I didn't like and what was bothering me about the job, my co-workers, and the unhealthy environment. Instead, however, I said that I wanted to explore a bigger city and to expand my opportunities. This was very well received, and helped maintain relationships with co-workers I left. You don't have to tell untruths, but it can be good to put a positive spin on your story.

Communicating with others
Leading on from this, two areas of consideration are how open we should be with others about leaving, and how to obtain support during the process. Would it make sense to tell many people about our leaving? If not, are there safe people we could share with who would provide support and encouragement? Are there mentors who can guide us and provide advice?

On the whole, my advice is: proceed with caution. You don't always get the response you might expect! Once you start announcing your decision to leave to others at your workplace, you are engaging in a fascinating social experiment in which individuals reflect their feelings to us. Although some people respond with, "Good for you!" and, "Congratulations!" we are also likely to receive responses that reflect the others' anxiety about our decisions.

When I left an academic job to work independently, some people (who had just been complaining about their jobs), said, "How can you leave academia? How can you become a consultant? Aren't you worried about [paying your bills, health insurance, finding work, surviving]?" These responses initially unsettled me, until I realized that they had nothing to do with me and that they in fact all reflected the other person's concerns. Some people are aware of this and say things like, "I could never do what you are doing. You are so brave." Others use humor. "Take me with you!" You will likely be put in a position of needing to respond to these reactions.

What's most important to remember is that their responses are about them, not about you. Still, their responses can be difficult to manage if you're already in a bit of a fragile state about leaving. Have the conversations anyway. As author Tim Ferris[1] said, "A person's success in life can usually be measured by the number of uncomfortable conversations he or she is willing to have." Bear in mind that you don't have to take on other people's anxieties about your choice.

People may react with surprise to your disclosure that you're leaving, such as, "I had no idea you were even thinking of leaving." Or they may nod knowingly and say, "Yes, I knew you were unhappy." These responses can be tinged with support, such as friends who immediately say, "I'm so happy for you!" or, "I know it was a hard decision, and I'm here for you." Telling people you are leaving may also bring their resentment, anger, or lack of support to the surface. There may be responses along the lines of, "But who will take care of me?" or even minimizing your contributions to date.

Many times when leaving, I am asked about what's next. Be aware that there is often a lot of judgment from others about your answer to this, and that these questions can be challenging when you're not sure of what's next. I moved to Oregon with my then-husband even though our marriage was rocky. When we finally split up, a friend said, "But you just moved across the country with him! You're broke, not finished with school, and you don't know anybody there! What will you do now?" Ouch. My friend provided a summary of all the things I was scared to death about, and it was challenging to hold it together and say, "Well, I'm not sure what's next, but I know this is the right decision for me."

When I left a job in Oregon for a similar position in New York City, several people felt I was being arrogant or "uppity" for moving to New York City. When I left a job to start my own consulting firm, several people said, "But how will you pay your bills? Isn't that risky? Where will you live?" Of course, others said in both situations, "I'm so happy for you — you will be fantastic and successful!" Those were the ones I chose to listen to most.

Through the course of my leaving experiences, and during interviews for this book, I found that many people are unhappy but quite reluctant to make a major change ("stayers"). Your announcement that you are leaving can cause significant dissonance to them, which they express in interesting and not always positive ways. Martha Beck writes about how in leaving the Mormon Church, she was essentially banned from previously close relationships, even with family members.[2] When I left the Army, several senior staff told me, "You'll never make it out there. You know you have to pay for your rent *and* your health insurance *and* your utilities separately – that's a LOT to manage!" (Wow.) Agung from Connecticut said that when he was asking his advisory board directions in which to take his company, one advisor said, "This is as good as it gets. Life is hard." That's not exactly what we look for in an advisor.

Some people say ridiculous things to manage their own anxiety. I met up with a former academic colleague (definitely a stayer) a few months after I left to start my consulting firm. When she asked how things were going, I let her know things were going well. She exclaimed, "Oh, I'm so glad to hear that you're not destitute on the side of the road!" I don't think she realized how that came across to me! Although it was a bit surprising and somewhat funny, we then went on to have a conversation about leaving and staying and she confessed she had wanted to leave several times but could never work up the nerve to pursue it.

This is where having your story and sticking to it is helpful. Find your mantra, such as "I'm happy with my decision," or "I appreciate your support" (even if they weren't especially supportive), or "I'm really looking forward to what's next" and stick with it. Remember, their responses are about them, not about you. But it's easy to get caught up in their responses, especially if they are people important to you, if they speak to your own anxieties, or if they are not particularly supportive.

My best example of a leaving story is when I leave a job. There are the people to tell first and in person, like my immediate staff, my immediate supervisor and other key people. This round is important because these people will start talking and will tell others. Sometimes you may want people to find out second-hand, so you tell someone you know will spread the news. A second round is people to tell in person or on the phone after the first round, and then perhaps a third one of email recipients. A final message can be sent after leaving to let people know it has happened.

For me, a leaving veteran, I find this process of thoughtful communication to be crucially important. It's important to me to maintain positive relationships as far as possible, and to be respectful of others. I consider how far in advance to let people know — too early or too late can both be logistically problematic or disrespectful. I carefully think through how to make different rounds of disclosure, how to have the conversation (e.g., in person, or via phone, email or social media). I always start by sharing the news with a few confidantes whom I know will be supportive.

Leaving is sometimes open, where everyone knows we are heading off to college in the fall, or leaving a temporary job at the end of the month. Open leaving in some ways forces us to deal mentally with the challenges of leaving: it's hard to deny we're leaving when everyone knows and asks us about it. It's also easier to obtain support, guidance, and advice. Sometimes, though, it means that in addition to managing our own internal processes, we have to manage others' issues about leaving, as described above. This can be even more acute in a work situation.

I once left a workplace before having secured the next job. For some colleagues, this was extremely anxiety provoking. They would stammer: "But what are you going to do? How will you live without a job? Aren't you worried?" Of course I was worried, but it wasn't helpful to have their anxiety to deal with on top of my own. Over the weeks before leaving, I learned to restate my intentions in the face of their anxiety and not to let their anxiety increase my own.

When leaving is not open, people can sometimes feel deceived, hurt, or angry that you hid something from them. Sneaking away in the night is sometimes warranted, such as if there is a threat of violence, such as a domestic or workplace abuse situation. Each of us has to determine how to manage the leaving process with others.

Acknowledge and start dealing with your feelings about leaving
Most people don't like this part. Others appreciate the assistance of a trusted friend, or a confidential journal, to work through these feelings. I'm not suggesting that in the midst of planning everything, you must spend a lot of time on your feelings, but it can be helpful to take a few moments to be honest with yourself about your (likely conflicting) emotions and to be easy on yourself.

What kinds of feelings come with leaving?

I could've done more/I'm satisfied with what I did. Leaving a marriage led me to feel I'd failed. I spent too much time thinking I could have done more to save the relationship, but when I pushed myself to identify what more I could have done, nothing came up other than, "Sacrifice my wants and desires." That helped me move toward realizing that although I was unhappy with the outcome, I did all I could to be a good partner and to support the relationship. Thinking about our role in this way helps identify where we might be feeling regret, or sadness, or dismay, or joy (or sometimes all of these!) at leaving.

My ex-wife and I had lived off my student loans while I was in school. It turns out that while she was controlling the checkbook, she was defaulting on my payments and buying things for herself instead. I realized something was wrong when we got a shut-off notice for the electric bill. When I asked her about it, she refused to show me the checkbook. When we divorced, I asked for her to repay some of the loans since she was using the money, but she refused. I decided to let it go. It was an expensive lesson, but I feel like I bought my freedom.

-Clark (New York City)

I will miss these people/I will not miss these people/I hate these people and never want to see them again. In my various leaving experiences, I have encountered mostly the former, some of the middle, and rarely the latter. Sometimes people I felt frustrated with or whom I didn't care for were surprisingly kind and compassionate about my leaving. Others whom I was close to told me flat out that they're not good at keeping in touch and that we probably won't talk again. Ouch. It's important to recognize your own feelings so that you can keep those separate from other people's reactions to your leaving, which are about them.

I want to keep in touch/I don't want to keep in touch. There's a cleanness to just splitting and not keeping up with the other. This is something that may be difficult for stayers to understand. When a leaver feels that restlessness and must leave, the next thought isn't always, "How can I best maintain the closeness of this relationship?"

John Steinbeck's *Travels with Charley in Search of America*[3] clarifies his steps of leaving for adventure:

When the virus of restlessness begins to take possession of a wayward man, and the road away from Here seems broad and straight and sweet, the victim must first find in himself a good and sufficient reason for going. This to the practical bum is not difficult. ... Next he must plan his trip in time and space, choose a direction and a destination. And last he must implement the journey. ... I set it down only so that newcomers to bumdom, like teen-agers in new-hatched sin, will not think they invented it.

Planning transition activities

Some kinds of leaving lend themselves to garnering support from others. Leaving a job, for example, whether desired by co-workers or not, may result in a goodbye party or after work drinks to celebrate moving on. Graduating from high school and leaving for college is lauded as a positive developmental step worthy of celebration, and even leaving an unpleasant relationship can inspire support from close friends who have observed our unhappiness up close. In some cases, there is less or even no support. Leaving home is an excellent example of when family and friends may feel a mix of emotions that can affect our excitement about our journey forward.

One note of caution: even with the best planning, things sometimes do not go as planned. As author William Gibson[4] said, "Scenarios have to be plausible, but reality is under no such constraints." Time spent planning and considering your preferences and options is not wasted, even when plans go awry. It will make you more confident to address whatever comes your way.

Chapter 8: Leaving

Change, when it comes, cracks everything open.

-Dorothy Allison[1]

Moving day! Last day at work! Last day of school! These are such bittersweet moments and so much happens at once. I love those moments when our heads are so full of thoughts and feelings and plans and memories and change that it seems as if they'll burst. There's nothing like the moment of leaving itself, although it can vary greatly.

Sometimes, leaving takes place in the night, without human interaction. In *The Runaway's Diary*,[2] teenager Cat describes her actual leaving as straightforward and simple: "It was easy this morning. Can't get over it. Thinking about doing something and doing it, that's different. But I just woke up, got dressed, got my stuff together and walked out. No one said a word."

Poet Audre Lorde[3] describes moving out after escalating arguments with family members:

I went to work, returned home after my family was asleep, and packed. What I couldn't carry I dumped into a sheet and dragged down the street and left at the foot of the steps of the police station. ... I left a cryptic note on the kitchen table which read, 'I am moving out. Since the causes are obvious, the results are well

known.' I think I meant it the other way around, but I was very
excited and very scared. I was seventeen years old.

Sometimes, leaving is accompanied by great fanfare, such as a going away party. It's nice to know people are wishing you well. When my ex-husband and I divorced on good terms, I proposed we have a Divorce Party to let others know about our mutual decision to go our separate ways. He thought it was morbid, and perhaps it was. (We didn't have the party.) Other times, we must muscle our way out at the last moment. For example, even when I gave six weeks' notice that I was leaving a job, the same people who had treated me poorly accused me of leaving them in the lurch (six weeks' notice!!) and asked me to stay longer to make it easier on them. (I did not.)

Finally, sometimes leaving is just fading away. Turkish playwright and novelist Mehmet Murat Ildan suggests, "Leaving a place, a person or a country silently and without any notice is a heroic and a noble way of teaching the importance of your presence to those who ignore your existence."[4]

When I was preparing to leave the military, I visualized driving away from the Army base and looking at it in the rear-view mirror. I imagined that scene so many times that I can still see it in perfect relief today: bright sun, desert sand, and the front gates of the base receding as I drive forward to freedom. The day I actually left, however, I didn't even look in the rear view mirror, and I didn't realize I missed my rehearsed moment until I was miles away. It doesn't matter, though. I like to think I was so focused on where I was going that it didn't occur to me to look back.

Regardless of how it takes place, in the moment of leaving you may feel unreal, unsettled, or as if you are hanging on a precipice. That's normal. As Cat in *The Runaway's Diary*[5] says, "When you think for a long time about doing something, something really big, then suddenly you realize that you are actually going to do it, it makes you feel shaky all over. Like, I look at that face in the mirror, and I don't even know it." Being able to tolerate feeling unsettled while moving forward is a sign of strength.

Let's slow this process down and take a look at all of its parts.

Enjoyment, accomplishment, and celebration

I think it's important to celebrate leaving, even if it's by yourself. It's nice when others are involved in a farewell party or lunch. Even if it's a painful separation, or a private one, some sense of ritual can go a long way toward helping you process a big change. It allows you to celebrate your choice to choose growth, to be brave, and to look forward to the future.

Remember of course that the party isn't always just about you. You are the guest of honor, but it also allows those who are being left behind to celebrate, to say their goodbyes and good-lucks, and to process that you're no longer going to have the same role in their lives as before, for good or for bad. As far as possible, it's good to choose your own celebration.

Ideally, have only people who are supportive there, and who can help you feel good about your next steps on your journey. If that's not possible, try to minimize time and energy on those who are not supportive. Consider strategies discussed in Chapter 7, *Preparation*, on deflecting other people's anxieties about your choices. Insist on celebrating your decision process and your courage, even if the leaving itself brings mixed feelings.

Zenglo, who left China in his twenties, said there was no special ceremony or goodbye party when he left China. He said, "My father gave me $42. And bought the tickets and suitcases and backpack. I was dirt poor. My family didn't have much money, so there was no party. It was almost like medieval times when you sent someone to the monastery. You just left."

Anxiety and fear

Thought you were done with anxiety once you are at the going-away party, or the courtroom, or the graduation stage? Nope. You now are likely to feel a flood of emotions. In addition to the positive emotions of enjoyment and accomplishment, for many of us, the finality of the Official Leaving Ritual (whatever that might be) brings back all the anxiety and fear we worked so hard to conquer. Perhaps the anxiety is about whether we are making the right decision (we are), or whether we can handle what comes next (we can), or whether the people around us will be okay after we leave (they will). We may start thinking of worst-case scenarios, such as if you have a car accident on the way to college, or if all your friends abandon you for leaving your hometown.

To manage these anxieties and fears, first remember that they're just thoughts. They're not real events. Second, notice what's going on, that your mind is getting a bit out of control. Next, try to deal with the issue itself, without piling on more judgment: you're already anxious, but there's no need to berate yourself for feeling anxious! Then examine the evidence. While it's possible your car might crash on the way to college, it's unlikely, given your careful driving habits. You've not caused a car accident before. Then try to increase your sense of control; for example, note that you are doing everything you can to drive safely and follow all precautions. You may also want to think of the worst-case scenario: even if you do get in a fender-bender, you'll likely be perfectly fine or at worst delayed slightly. Anticipate that you may feel anxiety and fear and identify ways to manage it so it doesn't detract from your joy.

Memories

Be aware that memories will come creeping or flooding in. Best to prepare for this, acknowledge them, and let them float on. To prepare during the last few weeks before leaving, I always think, "Soon I won't be taking this drive to work anymore," or, "This may be the last time I see this person," or, "I'll miss our special jokes." These memories can bring on a variety of feelings and may even change how you view your leaving. Like many other experiences during your leaving moment, it's important to let these memories come and go. It's also important to ensure that any memories that come up on the last day don't ruin the moment or change your resolve. For example, when I was leaving a partner, our last goodbye brought a flood of memories of good times, fun vacations, holding hands, and all kinds of goodness that made me feel so very sad. The thought did occur to me to change my mind, to reconcile, to try to recapture those positive feelings. But I knew all of the not-good stuff would come back too, and that breaking up was the right thing to do.

When negative memories come back, it may be tempting to give a primo parting shot or to tell that so-and-so what you really think of him. Although it may seem satisfying, this is rarely in your best interests. With people or situations that I found frustrating, I try extra hard to ensure that I find something positive. In every experience and in every relationship, I try to appreciate the path I've been on. When the memories come back, it's okay to remember both the good and the bad, and to let it go.

Logistics

Hopefully you've had an opportunity to prepare well, so you have a guide for your actual leaving (see Chapter 7: Preparation, for more on logistics). If it's possible to throw in a few perks for yourself while planning, that would be great. For example, when I left for a cross-country move, I arranged to spend the last night with a friend who surprised me with a goody bag of chips and snacks for the journey. What a joy! Another time when I left a challenging job, I planned ahead so that the day I left the job, I would have dinner with fantastic friends who would be supportive, whether I was excited, an emotional mess, or both!

Other logistics are more challenging. For example, in a divorce, there are logistics to manage which just can't be accomplished in a short amount of time. You may be able quickly to close joint bank accounts or to transfer the car title to one person's name. But six months later you may realize that your ex-spouse is still listed as your emergency contact. Or that your ex didn't tell a mutual friend that you separated, and you must share the news. Children may ask questions over and over as they struggle to adjust to new situations. Many of these logistics can be thought through in advance (see Chapter 7: Preparation). But some may pop up on the day. If this happens, don't panic. Make a note to deal with it later and go back to enjoying your moment.

Safety is always the priority. Depending on the urgency of the situation, such as if there is partner or workplace violence, you may not be able to plan further ahead than that. If you have time and if safety isn't an issue, allow yourself the time to daydream about what could be. Don't go down the rabbit hole of how things can go wrong; rather, think of all the ways in which your life can open up in wondrous ways.

Relief

Many people feel enormous relief that the hard part is over. The die is cast; there's no turning back. This is exciting! It can be challenging to feel relief after all this work to make the leaving happen. You've been focused on taking care of so many logistics and relationships and anxieties. Now you can relax a little.

I was at a university with a very driven student population, and my parents pressured me to keep going on to graduate school. At beginning of my senior year, I remember telling my parents I needed to put off law school and to work a year. I got tremendous pushback from them. I remember putting my foot down and saying no. I got a job at an international law firm in NYC as a paralegal. I quickly realized that law was not the right thing for me because it was just the wrong profession, the wrong people. I was so miserable.

Eventually what I did – I wouldn't recommend this – I left the job by post-it note. It was 11pm and I was so miserable and crying and I wrote on a post-it note, "Sorry, it's not for me," and I walked out. It was a very important point in my life. Although everything was stacked against me, I knew at the tender age of 22 that I had to leave that job.

-Eric (New York)

Even if it was a difficult decision or if you still feel ambivalent or if some people are not happy with your choices, it's still okay to feel relief. As with anxiety above, there's no need to berate yourself for how you feel, and no need to feel guilty because you feel relief about moving on. You may feel both relieved, and sad about leaving your friends/family/colleagues. Sometimes other people don't understand this – feeling relieved doesn't mean you don't also feel many other things. People can get upset because you feel relieved, or they can put you down about how you feel. There's no need for you to become upset by that. You feel how you feel. It's fine to feel how you feel. It will be okay. You are on your way to the rest of your life.

Overwhelmed
All of this — excitement, joy, anxiety, memories, logistics, relief — it's a lot to take in. And as much as you attribute those butterflies to excitement instead of anxiety, sometimes your body tenses up, your neck may become stiff and your stomach start to ache. When this happens, breathing is your best friend. Deep breath in, deep breath out. Repeat.

When you feel overwhelmed, pull yourself slightly away from the event, even if only mentally. Sit still and observe what is going on around you. Take photos in your mind of everything you see. Take actual photos, as that may relieve you of having to make small talk for a while. Walk slowly to get a glass of water, then walk back and have a seat. Go to the restroom and have a moment of solitude. Do what you need to do to have some space and take care of yourself until the overwhelm passes.

For me, the biggest overwhelm, the last gut-wrenching moment, is looking around the empty apartment or house. Maybe it's just the way I arrived, so it's like I was never there. I feel like it's a part of my mind I will have to amputate.
-Gerry (Ohio)

You may have prepared for this, but there's no way fully to prepare for everything you're feeling. This big jumble of feelings is a strong sign that you are fully alive.

Self-care

Hopefully self-care is an integral part of your leaving-day process. If not, go back to your list of logistics and add it back in. It's not only good for you to take care of yourself, it's scientifically supported! Self-care can include self-kindness (treating yourself with understanding and forgiveness), an awareness of your place in shared humanity (remembering this too shall pass and you're not alone), and mindfulness (appreciating the present moment and not getting lost down the rabbit hole of negativity). People who do these things are better off than those who don't.

It may be tempting to let those self-care items drop off your list if you get anxious or things get busy. I have heard so many times people say that they're too busy to meditate, or too stressed to do yoga. But that's the time they are most important! Even taking 30 seconds to breathe and to say something nice to yourself can be helpful to reset your stress meter. And especially if other people or reality start giving you a hard time, that self-care will be extremely important, and can even help you heal faster.[6] You'll be glad you did it.

The best-laid plans…

As in the rest of life, sometimes when leaving, *things do not go as planned*. What a wonderful opportunity to learn! Here is a story of things definitely not going as planned.

When I left in search of adventure in India, there were parts of the trip where I was not happy. I was early in my adventuring career, and when things didn't work out the way I thought they would, I became grumpy, and alienated my travel-mates with my negative attitude and complaints. Once, nine of us Westerners tiptoed between several hundred Indians watching a ceremony on the Ganges River to sit on wet marble on the riverside. To me, we were uncomfortably close and needed the space outside. About a half hour later, we changed our minds when the monsoons struck again, and everyone rushed into the area with the roof, now sitting knee-to-knee and shoulder to shoulder. I felt very claustrophobic being so close to strangers. Everyone made room so that no one was out in the rain, and the ceremony started up again. We exchanged smiles, and although I was physically uncomfortable, my discomfort faded quickly as I reveled in the togetherness, and the beauty of the ceremony transfixed me. Somehow, my expectations and grumpiness had been swept aside. During an afternoon when nothing went as planned – between the waiting, the rain, the physical discomfort – everything was magical.

Nowadays, I do more of my own planning because I know that I am not very patient when trip planners are disorganized. That also means

I miss out on unique opportunities like the Indian ceremonies unless I make a strong effort to put myself out there and explore. And I try to be less cranky regardless – that's just a good plan anyway.

When other things don't go as planned, it helps to have a sense of humor about them. Planes may get delayed, the car may not start, packages may get lost, people may melt down, *you* may melt down. It's all okay. Time will pass, and eventually – at some point perhaps far in the future – it will become funny.

Once the goodbyes are said, the judge has ruled, and you are on the train or in your car, or in a bus, or by yourself somewhere heading away or off to sleep, allow yourself to review the day. Let yourself look back at all the photos you took in your mind, walk through all the steps, evaluate what it took to get here. Let yourself *feel* the day. Feel your life shift in a major way. Feel the anticipation of what comes next. And enjoy it.

Moving frequently as a child increased my resilience and helped me get more comfortable meeting new people. I inherited my parents' adventurousness. Part of me craves staying in the same house forever, but having moved frequently, I know my home is in me.

-Katharine (New York)

I'm not recommending this, but sometimes people pick a fight right before they leave because in some ways it makes it easier to leave. I'm sure I was not the only teenager to experience increased arguments with my parents before leaving home. Imagine my surprise when I found out my mother had the same experience of escalating arguments with *her* parents before she left home!

Of course it's not usually intentional, but unfortunately it's common as both sides feel anxiety and sadness and possibly relief about one of you moving on. It's especially common if you know you're leaving and the other party doesn't know yet. Sometimes, these kinds of arguments are the only way people can move on, especially if they had a close and loving relationship previously.

Arguments to me are like a canary in a coal mine. More disagreements or more heated arguments than usual, whether with a partner, co-worker, or friend, sets off my early warning signal and makes me ask myself, "What's going on?" If I can stop for a moment to check in, I can usually identify the issue. I try to leave on good terms (although that's not always possible), so that I try and correct the issue. If we know we're leaving, that's often a good cue to *let things go*.

For example, I lived with a partner who expected me to keep up with his family events, such as birthdays and special occasions. His choice not to take responsibility for his own family was irritating to me and would make me angry sometimes. Once we knew we were separating, he continued in the same way, but my reaction to it was very different. So when he would say, "Could you call my mom to check on what time lunch is this weekend?" instead of getting angry, I would think, "There are only a few more times I will get to have lunch with his mom as the daughter-in-law. I'm choosing to enjoy lunch," and "I wonder what it will feel like in a few months when I only have to think about my *own* family?"

Picking fights also complicates the emotional issues associated with leaving. Over time, I've become more skilled at separating my internal sense of, "I need to leave" with unhelpful thoughts of, "Why isn't this person more x?" or, "If only this person would y, then I would stay."

Not helpful. Just like the macaroni and cheese example, it's not the fault of the macaroni and cheese that I changed. It's also helpful to remember at this point that you are moving on because it is in the interest of your greatest good. It is inevitable that you will make these decisions. So as the saying goes, "We can do this the easy way or the hard way." Why do it the hard way? Deal with your stuff, and don't take it out on other people. Be glad you had the experience and be glad you are moving on.

I am in a relationship now that is not good for me. My husband and I have different levels of ambition. I am working very hard and supporting us, but because of my culture, everyone gives him the credit for everything I do. It's also very difficult to divorce because of our religion; my mother and my pastor keep saying I should try to work it out. But I'm very unhappy. I am hustling to stay – to try to make both sides of the relationship work on my own. I can see the signs [the relationship] isn't working because in my heart I know it isn't adding value to my life.

-Bee (Malawi)

Chapter 9: Integration

You've done it. You've walked out of the divorce court, you're on your way home after your last day at the old job, or you're getting in the moving van to drive away from the old house. It really happened. You left. Now, once the adrenaline dissipates, it's time to begin the process of becoming the new you.

The immediate effects of a transition can be challenging. We may come home to an empty home, or arrive at college alone, knowing we must make new friends. We may wake up the morning after our last day at work thinking, "What have I done?" and, perhaps, "Where's my next paycheck coming from?" After a breakup, many of us go through a carbohydrate binge, ice cream extravaganza, or hibernation – and there's nothing wrong with that. Or perhaps we develop a renewed focus on getting healthier. I started running after I was divorced (partly to counteract the ice cream). Sometimes it can be hard to stick with our plan, and sometimes we can slip up and go visit our ex or backslide into perhaps wishing we hadn't left.

For the first month after leaving my girlfriend of seven years, I was euphoric. I was giddy. I was free. After a month, I thought, "Oh no! What have I done? She was so good to me. I want her back!" Then I would remember it was better we weren't together. It turns out she would think the same things sometimes too. Thankfully, whenever I was in the thought process of wanting to get back together, she was on the side of not getting back together, so we never got back together. And now, I'm relieved – I know I did the right thing.

-Karen (Sydney)

Importance of rituals

Leavers like me often use rituals to mark the transition and finalize the change. When I've left a job, for example, one of my rituals is to update my resume so it reflects that the old job is over and something new has started. For me, this gives a measure of finality and underlines that I'm no longer at my previous place of employment. I also contact any remaining professional colleagues to announce the change and pack up any files from the old job. And (because I'm such a nerd) I modify my folder structure on my laptop to indicate that job is no longer front and center, it's in the past.

Moving house provides many opportunities ritually to "let go" of the former home. There's the first walk around the new neighborhood, stopping in any restaurants or shops and having the first conversation saying, "I just moved here." Inevitably they will say, "Where did you move from?" and you get an opportunity to practice saying, "I *used to live* in x." After we moved when I was in third grade, I remember memorizing my new phone number before I headed to school for the first time because I knew it was important. We don't always change phone numbers when we move, but memorizing your new address, and developing a story about why you moved to the new place is a wonderful way to begin integrating your leaving.

Leaving a relationship also provides new firsts. The first evening settling into your home without your ex, or into your new home by yourself, can feel sad and exciting and comfortable all at the same time. The first holidays without the ex are sometimes challenging. The first Thanksgiving without my ex-husband's family was very difficult, especially knowing they were celebrating together just across town without me. A friend invited me to spend it with her family, and I'm sure I looked like a zombie (I definitely felt like one!). At one point a cousin of hers started talking with me and said as I teared up, "I was divorced once. The first holiday is always the hardest. Just get ready for your life to get SO much better." I have always been thankful for his kindness.

Choosing to leave means there is anxiety because you have to make a choice. Some people don't like doing it, because they don't want that anxiety. You have to leave something to get something. Most people want to keep everything and gain, but that's against the movement of life.

-Sandra (Rio de Janeiro)

There's also the fun of creating new rituals. Having breakfast at home after leaving a job. Creating new holiday traditions. Finding coffee shops and restaurants in your new neighborhood. And as we continue to explore our new lifestyle, the process of integrating our life story is continuing, consciously or unconsciously.

The four components to integration
My interviews suggested four really important components to integrating your past after making a major change.

1. The experience you left will always be a part of you, and it helped make you who you are.
There will be moments where you think back to your former home, spouse, job, or religion, and have strong feelings. You may have feelings of regret because you miss your friends. You may feel guilty because you left. You may remember the happy times with your former spouse. It's important to let these feelings come up, but not to get stuck in them. The experiences you had will

always be a part of your life, and they'll always define part of who you are. They will also help you recognize who you are.

Because of the experiences I've been through about leaving jobs – getting so frustrated, yelling at my boss, leaving by post-it note — I think moving forward I won't have to hit rock bottom to know when it's time to leave. I will be able to recognize it and move forward. The first few times I left, it probably came from a place of rock bottom. It wasn't as urgent to leave until I hit rock bottom. When I think about it, it makes me cringe. It was an uncomfortable and unhappy time of my life, and I was scared to leave until it got so bad that I blew up.

If you've never been through it, you'll probably take it to rock bottom, but I think it's better not to get to that place. Now I have the tools to catch it before it gets there. In my new career, I probably won't let it get all the way there before I know things need to change.

-Eric (New York)

You really do learn from experience.

When I think about being married, I reflect fondly on falling in love, getting married, and the happy times my ex-husband and I had together. It was absolutely the right thing to do to get married. I enjoyed the adventures we had together, I love his family, and I'm a much better person now than I would have been had we not been married. At the same time, I think of the ways in which we started working at cross-purposes because we wanted different kinds of lives, and about the way we grew to treat each other differently, and I know getting divorced was also absolutely the right thing to do when the time came.

At first I was ashamed of being divorced. I felt it was a sign that I had failed, or a negative mark on my "permanent record," perhaps because I was one of the first in my friendship group to get divorced. But as time has passed, I no longer feel ashamed. I have some bittersweet feelings, that it was a lovely experience and that it's too bad we weren't able to stay together. But now he and I are both living the lives we wanted, and which we never could have had if we had stayed together. I am very glad that we loved each other enough to let each other go.

When I look back on leaving my ex-husband, I realized how much fear kept me stuck with him. You can look at the evidence intellectually and counter the fear and the causes logically, but I think there has to be a development of self-love in there. Because where there is love, there is no fear. Getting to that love is the hard part: forgiving ourselves, loving life, loving ourselves. I had to love myself before I was able to leave him. Leaving him was a pivotal moment because it was a big shift in how I saw myself.

-Linda (New York)

Just as it's important to allow yourself to feel as you're making a decision, it's important to allow yourself to reflect back on all that happened. You had one life where things were a certain way, and now your life is completely different because you chose to leave. Or you think about your life differently because you chose to stay. Wow! You did this. You made this happen. The process of thinking through what you want from life, what should do, and the impacts of your decision made you a stronger and wiser person. Take the time to look back and appreciate the complexity of the experience you just went through.

2. You were courageous to choose your life.

Another facet of integrating your experience is that you were brave enough to choose your life. Not only is it okay to do something for yourself, but it's also important to normalize the process of making difficult decisions and standing by the consequences. Otherwise, you're just floating through life.

I know it's important for me to rely on myself. It's not selfish. I do something because I think I need to do it. I feel it in my heart, my life, my gut. It's good for my own well-being. And if the decision is for me, and I do no harm, then it's the right decision. Of course, sometimes I need to take one for the team, for my family, or for others. I think people who don't want to make decisions about their lives really fear to be themselves.

-Charles (South Africa)

Hilda, a gerontologist from Kenya, said, "I always go day to day just reacting to life. I love my family, but it seems like every now and then I realize another year has gone by, or another two years, and I think, 'What is life really about? How do I want my life to be?'" After our conversation, Hilda started moving forward by having a serious conversation with herself about what she wants from life. I have no doubt she will identify what she wants and move toward it.

When coach and author Martha Beck left the Mormon Church, her world turned upside down.[1] As she wrote in her book, *Leaving the Saints*, she has no regrets:

My defection from Mormonism changed me ... I'm starting to believe that my homing instinct will guide me back anytime I consult it, from anywhere in creation. I think that may be the reason for this whole terrifying, excruciating mortal existence: To wander away from home, then find the way back, so many times we learn from our toes up that no matter how far afield we may stray, we can always, always, always get there from here.

When you have left something or someone, or when you thought about leaving but decided to stay, you have had that moment of reckoning where you decided, explicitly or implicitly, that where you were was not what you wanted and that you wanted more. That is amazing! That is brave! That is courageous! That is awesome!

3. You made the right decision

I firmly believe that the decisions I make are the right ones. Does that mean I am always right? As much as I'd like to be, no, I'm not always right. But I am willing to act on my decisions, to take a calculated risk and move ahead. That, for me, makes the decision the right one. It's not a question of right/wrong, but of expansion and growth. Like Susan Jeffers' "No Lose Model,"[2] no matter what we choose, we have amazing opportunities to develop and learn.

Looking back on getting divorced, some bits are sad, but I don't regret any of it. It is what it is. Sometimes there comes a moment where you just have to take that leap. And things do work out. Even though you don't think they are going to. Whether you have to work harder or get another job or get another three jobs, it does work.

-Teresa (England)

When I was in training to be a therapist, I went to a training program by a well-known child psychologist. He provided instruction on how to work therapeutically with children using play therapy, which is where the child directs play and the therapist uses the opportunities presented to help the child work through his or her challenges. Toward the end of the day, a therapist in the audience asked, "What happens if in the middle of playing, the child hits you?"

The psychologist smiled and said, "I believe I'm *not* going to get hit." There was an awkward silence and some nervous laughter in the room. The questioner persisted and chuckling a little said, "Okay, but what if you get hit?" He responded by saying, "I believe I'm *not* going to get hit." This went back and forth a few times and finally the psychologist said, "Okay, have I ever been hit by a child in a therapeutic setting? Of course. But I *believe* I'm not going to get hit. Every time, every child, I *believe* I'm not going to get hit. Because I'm the grownup in the room, and if I can't believe the child can control himself, how can I expect him to believe he can control himself?"

This story has stuck with me for many years, long after I completed my training and even after I left being a therapist. For me, I internalize that I *believe* I make the right decisions. I am thoughtful, I am reasoned, I am ethical and empathic, and I believe each time I've left something or someone, it's been the right decision. I believe that each time, I made the best decision I could, given what I knew at the time and the circumstances I was in. Could I have handled things differently? Of course.

Cat, from Marilyn Harris' book *The Runaway's Diary*,[3] recognized after a year on the road that she had changed substantially:

Because no matter what ... all that's important is to realize that you are alive, and that one day you will be dead. ... Because if you know you are alive, really know it, then you can do exactly everything.

One time I found myself back in a city I had left, having a drink alone at a bar while waiting to meet a friend. I looked around at the day-drinkers and had a moment of loneliness: What happened to my life? I thought back through why I moved to that town (to save a relationship, which was not savable) and why I left (job opportunity, ambition, and need for change). I thought of all I learned while I lived there, including independence, confidence, how to go after what I want, how to be a professional and manager, how to get things done, how to find my place in relationships with others ... the list goes on. Further, I realized these decisions were my choices. I realized that even when I may have felt like I didn't have much choice, I chose how to proceed. I *chose* this life.

4. It's okay to have feelings.

It's okay to feel sad, frustrated, unhappy, giddy or excited. Or sometimes all at once – even if others don't feel comfortable with this. Sarah from Portland told me, "After my divorce, I was thrilled. I had been so unhappy for so long. And some of my friends and relatives felt that I should have been more reserved and unhappy. But by the time the divorce was finalized, it had really been over for a long time."

As reality sinks in, unhelpful beliefs can be activated. These may include:

- I'm a failure
- I'm unlovable
- I'll never find love again
- I'll never find another job
- No one understands me
- I'm a bad parent
- I'm too old/out of shape/ugly/unlovable to ever find someone else.

There are strategies to help address these unpleasant feelings. A strategy that is NOT helpful is to try and fight or deny the feelings, or to belittle yourself because of your emotions. The feelings are there for a reason. What can you learn from them?

Although these feelings may seem very real, they needn't be permanent. A good way to approach them is to feel them and let them go. As in meditation, you let the feeling exist, you acknowledge it, and you let it float away.

Another strategy is to replace a negative belief with another, more positive option. Instead of thinking, "I just left – why can't I get anything right?" a more helpful approach is, "I'm so glad I keep making the right decisions to take my life in the right direction." Instead of, "I'll never find love again," think, "Wonderful love is waiting for me as long as I continue to stay on my right path." Louise

Hay and Susan Jeffers are experts with ideas of how to frame positive self-talk. (See the For Further Reading section).

The fact that a person loved me once is proof that it can happen again. Though it is not a guarantee, this proves it is possible. From there, I do whatever is in my hands to make sure I deserve what I want, and I hope for the best.

-Hugo (Colombia)

Guilt is particularly common when leaving. For example, people may feel guilty leaving others behind, or having an opportunity that others don't have, or being able to see and take a chance when others can't. They may be aware that something special is happening in their lives, and yet feel guilty at this. If you find yourself besieged with guilt, it is first important to see if the guilt is yours, or if it is what someone else wants you to feel. People who don't like being left behind can be very good at trying to make you feel guilty. (Especially our parents – remember, they push our buttons so well because they installed them!) If at all possible, let guilt go. It is not serving you.

Many people I interviewed said they felt like failures because it took them so long to realize that they needed to leave the situation. Abusive situations, unpleasant work situations, situations where they were not supported or encouraged. I admit: I have felt like this as well, such as when I stayed in a relationship two years past its sell-by date. I've also realized in retrospect that when things went wrong, no matter how much effort I put into trying to make them right, it didn't work because it *wasn't up to me alone* to make it right. When I feel this myself and when I hear this from others, I have compassion. We all make decisions we need to make when we need to make them.

There's no benefit in going over what should have been, except to learn from it and move on.

Lin Manuel Miranda's musical *In the Heights* has a bittersweet moment when an immigrant father who didn't finish high school addresses his college-bound daughter and says that this is where she does better than him, because she can see a future he can't.

Sometimes people use their feelings and experiences to help others.

After I left my ex-wife, the hardest thing to say out loud was, "This was abuse," because I'm a strong badass who doesn't take shit from people. And yet I was the victim of abuse. I feel it's important that people see that someone who acts like me and who looks like me can be a victim. My ex-wife never laid a hand on me but mentally she beat me to a pulp. Outwardly our relationship looked okay, but it wasn't. It became a really important part of my world to minister to other people going through the same thing. Because when you've gone through an emotionally abusive relationship, you see the signs, you hear the phrases people use because they came out of your own mouth.

-Clark (New York City)

Feel the feelings, let them go, and move forward into making our world a better place.

Keep moving forward.
Having decided to leave or to stay, it's time to move on. As mentioned above, it's important to take the time to process the changes that have

happened since that first glimmer of awareness that things could be different. But it's also vital to get to the business of living the life you want.

Remember Katrina who moved from San Antonio to New York City? She said that in San Antonio, she felt a gnawing in her gut that the walls were closing in on her because she was gay. She felt she had to start her true life, and that her true life was in New York City. She often shares stories of growing up in San Antonio, its annual *Fiesta* celebration, how much she misses her family, and how much she loves it when they visit. She even occasionally talks about moving back to San Antonio. But she always returns to the fact that New York City is where she wants to be. "San Antonio will always be my home. But New York is where my life is." She has integrated those pangs of missing her family, but keeps in touch through visits, phone calls, watching every Spurs game, and following local San Antonio news. She's become someone who's making her way in New York City, and she's happy about that.

Why do people think they don't deserve to be happy? I don't mean living in a mansion, helicopter, rock-star happy. Just day-to-day happy. Some people think they should suffer. Perhaps it's part of the founding U.S. culture of Protestantism, which suggests that working hard and suffering is the way to enlightenment. Of course pain is part of life. But as the Buddha says, suffering is optional. To which I add, suffering is not often useful, and very rarely fun.

As a leader, I found that many people are so unhappy at work. They complain about how things are. They don't want to take steps to change the situation, because they feel that nothing will actually improve. When changes do start, they complain about those, and then when things are better, they find something else to complain about. Early on, I felt this was a reflection of a shortcoming of my own – that I couldn't fix the workplace enough to make people happy. The more I got to know such people, however, I realized that I can't make them happy, and furthermore, some of them don't want to be happy. There's an odd satisfaction in being unhappy, being able to complain endlessly and to blame others for their situation. I'm not like that. I can't be like that. Of course, I can complain with the best of them. But I also am very interested in making changes and in making the situation better.

Others come from a long line of suffering. "Our grandparents were poor. Our parents struggled, and so we must struggle or we are somehow negating their experience." Again, parents are good at instilling these thoughts in us unintentionally. If you believe that life is hard, then you are likely to have a hard life because if it's not hard, you're not truly alive.

For a while, I believed something that I thought was a positive belief: I am someone who overcomes obstacles. That was great, but it also made my life a series of obstacles — once I overcome them, then I'm really living! It didn't take long to realize that, proud as I am of my ability to overcome obstacles, I do not want a life filled with them. I'm not advocating a life of sloth and undeserved luxury. But I am suggesting that we choose to be happy and to do things we enjoy.

In my clinical psychology training, I learned how to implement cognitive behavioral therapy for depression. The program had a significant component called "pleasant activities." The goal was to help patients identify positive events to help boost their enjoyment of life. Patients could track their mood along with the pleasant activities and identify (hopefully) that completing the activities was associated with improved mood. We cautioned the patients that the process wouldn't work if they picked "special" activities that are very pleasant but usually infrequent (like going to a concert or amusement park).

Instead, we encouraged them to identify everyday joys, like taking a walk, spending time with someone you care about, or reading a good book. As we progressed, I found that I started identifying activities that I enjoyed: hot tea with milk and sugar, curling up with a good book, dancing to music in my living room, seeing flowers in bloom, and looking at pictures of the ocean. Then the point of the intervention became clear. It is partly about increasing the number of pleasant activities you are doing; but it's also largely about *noticing* how much you enjoy the activities you're *already doing*. This was revolutionary to me. I had studied therapeutic interventions for several years by then, and I had read a great deal about how "life is how you look at it" but I had never fully grasped it until then.

Do we get what we're looking for?
    I think we do.
    I know I do.

I believe there are three truths of leaving:
- Things will not go exactly as planned.
- It will utterly and completely be worth it.
- It will change your life in amazing ways.

But you don't have to take my word for it!

A happy confluence of events resulted in a free day on a work trip, allowing me to zip around Sedona, Arizona, in a convertible Corvette. I followed a dirt road in Red Rocks State Park to an amazing vista. I sat down to meditate, but after a few minutes of blissful silence, I was accosted by sloppy brown Labrador kisses. The dog's owner, Geoff, ambled up, and we started talking. He explained that he was on a road trip from Vancouver, Canada, through Idaho, Washington, Oregon, California, and now Arizona. He was on Month 4. He said that in Canada, he felt that he was spinning his wheels and experiencing existential angst about the purpose of life. "And then I hit the road," he said, "and I haven't thought about it once." He said that being on the road helped him focus on what is important. "I'm just here to be who I can be. I've had more important connections with humans on this trip than I've had for a long time at home, and half of them – I don't even know their names. I spent years in Canada just working and toiling, and now I feel like I'm actually living life."

Don't let others distract you from what you're seeking.
In Chapter 7: Preparation, we looked at communicating with others – how to inform them we were going, and how to handle their anxieties especially when these were projected onto you. It's highly probable that you will have to return to this question as your leaving journey progresses. Making sense of your leaving experiences might be difficult if you listen to others' opinions about your choices. People might ask why you left or call you a quitter. They might suggest you don't have persistence, or that when the going gets tough, you split. They may even suggest that you should have stayed in the situation due to honor, valor, commitment, obligation, or some other reason. This is where you may need to re-examine your boundaries and decide how far you allow others to intrude with their opinions.

The truth is: you did what you needed to do. You made the best choice for you given what you knew at the time. Other people's opinions don't matter. Perhaps you weighed your options, thought through what you should do, examined your feelings, and decided leaving was the best choice. Perhaps you got up one day and said, "I can't take this anymore!" and left. Of course, you should try your best to do no harm. But let's say you are living at home with family members who treat you terribly. Are you obligated to stay? I don't think so. Let's say you married someone who ended up cheating on you, or significantly changing the terms of the relationship without asking you, or even heaven forbid, abusing you in some way. Hm. Should people be held to a commitment "'til death do us part" when they're clearly miserable?

My view is that it's okay to let go. I propose thoughtfulness, not impulsiveness. And to try and hold to the aim of not hurting anyone if possible. But someone who continues to feel extremely upset because you left your hometown to achieve your dream career doesn't really get a lot of sympathy from me. Of course it's okay for them to be upset. But hopefully the greater part of their heart is happy for you and supports you going off, being bold, and achieving your dream. That the loss they feel of you leaving is not as important as you feeling like you are doing what you need to do. And anyone who tries to make you feel like crap for leaving to achieve your dream isn't worth the time to argue with them.

For example, there may be an unstated obligation that, "Everyone in our family stays in this town. It's okay to go away to college if you want to do that, but the expectation is that you come back to settle down and raise a family." Note that "settling down and raising a family" is not an optional idea. It is *what we do*. In this model, anyone who doesn't return to the town and have children is viewed as violating this unwritten, likely unstated, rule about "what we do." And if you decide to move to the city, or travel the world, or not have children, or do any number of things that are not comfortable for your family (or maybe community) members, then you will get judged. They will say you are uppity, too big for your britches, have no sense of family, etc. all kinds of mean nasty things. They say these things to cover their sense of being upset you left, and because you chose to not do the things they did and the things they know. I have empathy for those feelings. If all you've known is one thing, and your child, sibling, or best friend does something totally different that's out of your bailiwick, then that can be threatening. And by its nature it forces you to think outside of yourself and your world. It makes you think, "Maybe there's a bigger world out there. This person wants to be a part of that bigger world. Should I?"

Leaving has been in my physiology since I was a child. We moved from California to Minnesota when my dad lost his job. I sobbed and sobbed. My grandmother held me and told me I'd meet new friends. I said, 'I don't want new friends! I want my old friends!' Maybe through those experiences I figured out a way to cope and deal with people differently. That's when I started keeping people at arm's length.

-Heather (California)

For me, I am afraid I wasted a lot of energy to move from house to house, place to place, job to job. When I think of the money I've spent on packing, moving vans, setting up a new house, getting rid of furniture that wouldn't work with the new place, all the time I spent looking for apartments, and buying curtains, furniture, and supplies for the new place. All the emotional energy thinking about leaving, deciding whether to leave, moving, and getting to know new friends, new neighborhoods, new rules at work, new colleagues, new projects. That is a lot of time and money and energy. At the same time, I look back upon my experiences, and although I would not have planned to leave like I did, every single leaving experience makes sense to me. Why I left this job, why I left this partner, why I moved across the country. They all individually make sense.

How do we leave better? Leaving lets people know we're independent and that we make our own decisions. This can sometimes be upsetting to them as it can trigger their feelings of dependence, abandonment, or inadequacy. I think the key is to express independence in a way that clarifies that I am seeking to become my best self, and which encourages others to be their best selves as well. I think we can present a sense of independence that says less, "I don't need you," and more, "We are still connected."

We believe without question almost everything we learn as children, stumble into the many potholes and pitfalls that mar any human endeavor, stagger around blindly in pain and outrage, then slowly remember to pay attention, to listen for the Silence, look for the Light, feel the tenderness that brings both vulnerable to wounds and communion with the force that heals them. ... If you [lose your way], pain will remind you to find your path again. Joy will let you know when you are back on it.

-Author Martha Beck in *Leaving the Saints*[4]

Leaving an impossible situation is a good thing, but it doesn't mean the impossible situation was good or that there's not a cost associated with it. I believe we are all yearning to reconnect with nature and with our purpose, to connect to our own power. We all can learn thoughtfulness about the process of leaving or staying, what drives us, what excites us, what moves us, what we want to do with our lives, and what delights us. You *will* make the right decision.

Part 3

Chapter 10: When Leaving Isn't Your Choice or When You Can't Leave

I was director of organizational development and human resources for a company with offices in North and Central America. I was leading a confidential project to lay off 10% of the workforce. I worked on this project with only my boss and the finance lead for months. Everyone who was getting laid off had to be notified on the same day, at the same time, across multiple countries. I worked so hard on this project. On the day of the project, I brought my team together with my boss to have a short meeting to prepare. We had all of the meetings scheduled, and there was security at each site. It was a good meeting. My boss then asked if I could stay with him for a few minutes. And also asked another direct report to stay. My boss was very calm. He said: "Zenglo, it's a bad day for you. You're also on the list for today. Your position is being eliminated." It turned out that my direct report had all the documents ready and showed me the separation agreement, the severance, and all the documents for me to sign. Of course I knew the documents because I put all of this together. I reviewed the documents, packed everything, and left. That was about 8:40am.

-Zenglo (Texas)

We've discussed extensively how to assert your agency and make your own decisions about whether to stay or leave. As this exceptionally callous behavior from Zenglo's company highlights, the flip side of this is when others make that decision and leave you behind. It may be that a lover walks out on you, your spouse decides to divorce you, your child leaves home, your boss fires you, or a friend ghosts you. Of course there's the ultimate being left: when someone dies, leaving you forever. Not everyone will be in Zenglo's work situation, of being forced to dig their own work grave, as it were. However, some of the most painful leaving situations that people described to me involved being forced to leave against their will or being involuntarily left behind. This chapter explores ideas about being left and how it can change your experience as a leaver or a stayer.

Being forced to leave can be deeply hurtful, as Zenglo's example shows. We can get fired summarily from a job. We may be asked to "resign by mutual agreement," or be forced out by a hostile work culture and unsympathetic colleagues. Some of us have been kicked out of our homes by parents or partners. Some of us have been excommunicated from our religion, or had a friend tell us the friendship was over.

In all these situations, our agency is impaired. We don't have control over what is happening in our lives, which makes everything feel even more out of control. Mourning takes on a larger role when leaving isn't in our control, because we must mourn not only the loss of the friend/partner/job but also the loss of our agency in being able to make our own choices and decide our future for ourselves.

In this chapter, I'd like to identify what happens when we get the information that we are being left, and then how we can adjust to these changes once they've happened.

Involuntary leaving

Almost all of us have experienced that sinking feeling when it becomes clear that we're confronting an involuntary leaving situation. Sometimes it's dramatic, like a punch in the gut, as when Zenglo was completely blindsided by being laid off because of a heartless work ethic after he had just completed a long and laborious project in good faith. Sometimes there's a slow fading away. Let's talk about how these experiences are different. Being blindsided is the most dramatic and shocking way of being left. You come home from work to find your spouse in bed with someone else, or to a note saying, "It's over." Your boss calls you in unexpectedly. Shock may be swiftly followed by anger. We may struggle simultaneously with questions like:

- What just happened?
- What went wrong?
- How long did the other person know this was coming?
- Who else knew about this?
- How could I have been so blind?
- Was all this my fault?
- What will I do now?
- What will I tell people?

Any one of those questions could be overwhelming and managing them all at once – often while reeling from the impact of the news – is extremely challenging.

I had a traumatic first relationship from when I was 16 years old until 27 years old. I held on with my fingernails to that relationship, always thinking, "Don't leave me!" He left anyway. I made a conscious decision to never be vulnerable to anyone else – until now. Now I'm 55 years old, I just got married, and I love him more than I thought possible.

-Roberta (Connecticut)

We are all familiar with the trope of the mid-life crisis. A person wakes up one morning in his 30s or 40s (or 50s) and decides this is not the life he wants and that he wants to reclaim his youth. Cue purchase of a sports car, erratic behavior, leaving family, and dating much younger people (or at least trying to). Of course, I do not promote abandoning one's family. I do, however, promote being thoughtful about how satisfied we are with our lives and taking steps to increase our satisfaction. James Hollis speaks eloquently about making difficult decisions in mid-life, in books such as *The Middle Passage: From Misery to Meaning in Mid-Life* and *Finding Meaning in the Second Half of Life.*[1]

The loneliness of being in a relationship with someone who has checked out and left without telling you is very painful indeed. It feels worse than if the person just left outright. Sometimes we physically leave because the other person has emotionally or mentally left us first. This is still painful and has the added strain of us needing to be the one to break the ties and do the leaving that is seen publicly. That makes the other person leaving us that much more painful. Sometimes there is an understanding that the other person has emotionally left but wants to continue to receive the benefits of being in a partnership, such as having companionship at social events, splitting costs, snuggling up, or receiving care when sick.

Depending on your interests, you may decide it suits you to stay in a somewhat diminished relationship. Or you may find such imbalance profoundly dissatisfying, and view your partner as one of life's takers. You may feel it is damaging because it breaks the social contract that we take the good with the bad in a relationship, and are committed to be fair toward each other. In those cases, anger and resentment toward the person perceived to be violating the social contract can be a powerful impetus to break off the relationship.

We are likely to feel that the other person imposed on us and took advantage of us, and at some point, we need to deal with this. And while it was probably never really about us, we still can end up feeling like a dope. Few constructs are more damaging in U.S. culture than to be thought of as a "chump," even (or especially) if we think that about ourselves.

"Ghosting" is a colloquial term originating in the early 2000s used to describe a cutting off of contact without warning, often in a romantic relationship. The person you were in a relationship with just disappears. They don't respond to calls, texts, or any other communication. People describe the experience as devastating, especially if there were no warning signs the person was uncomfortable. Here's an illustration.

An ex-girlfriend had a close friend, Will, who was accepted into a very prestigious graduate school program in a nearby state. They had known each other about five years and worked out together several times a week, celebrated birthdays together, and hung out all the time. My ex and I celebrated Will's grad school acceptance with him. We hosted a going-away party for him and gave him a morning take-off gift bag full of goodies for the drive. We were so excited to hear about how school went, and about his future successes ... except that we never heard from him again. My ex was devastated. She called and emailed, but never got a reply. She never heard from him again, and she never got any closure. It was completely inexplicable and very sad. We still don't know what happened with Will, but sometimes people ghost others because they don't want to have the difficult conversation to end the relationship. Unfortunately, this is so difficult for the person left behind, whether a romantic partner or a friend.[2]

People who have left a religion, political party, or some other organization, often describe the experience as feeling like they were abandoned first. People have left their church because they felt it abandoned the tenets that were thought to be held dear.

Leaders who professed to love their flock and who preached lovingkindness, attentiveness, and forgiveness, reacted to challenges by attacking, undermining, and shaming those who dared complain. There's a similar dynamic when people leave bullying bosses or abusive relationships.

Dealing with involuntary leaving

Much leaving consists of a slow process of identifying what you might like to do, how you feel about each step, and taking time to think though everything before making a decision to share with people and to act. Being left suddenly involves the reverse of this. There's no time for consideration, and the power is taken out of your hands. When you are left, the first step is to identify any immediate actions that need to be taken, then let people know, then to process what happened. I'll walk you through these steps below.

Breathe. First, take some deep breaths. You can do this.

Identify the issues. Next, identify what the issues are that may all be screaming at once in your mind. These may be all the questions above and more. Write them down if you need to. You may need to move quickly, in which case, just make a working list for now, and then revisit it later when you have more leisure. Make a list of your worries as well to help clear some space in your head. Some examples are listed below. Others are listed in Chapter 7: Preparation, under logistics.

Start prioritizing, with safety first. Although our tendency is to focus on the "What went wrong?" type of questions, the priority is immediate safety for yourself and others. Ensure that you and all others, especially children or anyone who is vulnerable, is physically safe from harm. This could include taking children to their grandparents' home so they can be safe for a few days, packing up the essentials, and physically getting out of the area if you need to.

Secure property, finances, and other logistics. Once you are sure of people's safety, identify what needs to be done to secure your property and address immediate financial issues. These might be things like closing joint accounts, hiring a lawyer, or changing the locks.

Find help. Identify an ally who can give you both practical and emotional support. This is someone who will not fall apart upon hearing your news but is able to help you *get things done* that need to be tackled right now. There will be plenty of time for emotional processing. A friend who can help at this point is extraordinarily valuable and can help ensure you've taken the immediate actions necessary to keep yourself and your property protected. After this, it may take weeks or months to work through financial issues, where you will be living, legal paperwork, and so on. During this time, it's imperative to take it easy on yourself and to continue to get nonjudgmental support.

Manage your emotional response. Finally, once life begins to feel at least sort of manageable again, you can begin the process of managing your emotional response to the situation, letting other people know, and moving on. Your emotional response to being left may be similar to Elizabeth Kubler-Ross's five stages of grief: denial, anger, bargaining, depression, and acceptance. These tools are not necessarily linear but may be helpful as we understand and work through our grief.

When someone leaves, you may feel betrayal (I thought you'd always be here), a sense of unwanted change (I liked my life the way it was), a sense of loss (I no longer have this person in my life), possibly a sense of jealousy (I wish I had that opportunity, or at least he is getting out of here), grief (about what might have been or could have been), and feelings about the person who left you or kicked you out (anger, wishing them well or ill).

When a close relative passed away, I felt so abandoned. Even though I knew it wasn't his fault, I was still upset that he left me. It took a long time to recover.

-Tom (New York City)

It's natural to feel these emotions — to feel betrayed even if it wasn't the other person's fault, or to feel jealousy or anger. It's fine to feel a mix of contradictory feelings at the same time. Grief is not tidy. Let's look at how to start working through those feelings in a way that helps you move forward.

Begin to share your story with others. At some point other people will begin to find out what happened, or you will need to let them know. What you share with people does not need to be the gut-wrenching, unvarnished truth. You may want to share more detail with a few close friends or family members — how betrayed, hurt and devastated you feel. Otherwise, for those not in your immediate close circle, it's important to consider what you want to share. I'm not suggesting that you tell untruths, but you can choose how you want to present information. For example, you may have found your spouse in bed with someone else. You do not have to tell everyone this. It is perfectly acceptable to share with co-workers that, "Things just didn't work out between us," or, "We had different priorities," both of which are true. This version of the story could also save you significant embarrassment and humiliation. Protect your dignity and your privacy.

It's up to you to determine what you want to keep private. Remember that when you make things public, you are opening yourself up to people's comments, questions and advice, which you may not want. When a partner withdrew from me to the extent that I ended up leaving, I lost one friend who said, "You should have just stayed – You could have made it work!" Her response suggested she wasn't really listening to me or connecting with me. She wasn't able to provide the support that I needed. It was unsettling. I responded by saying, "This was a very difficult situation, you don't have the whole story, and I would like your support." Unfortunately, she never called back after that, to see how I was doing or to reconnect, and our friendship faded away.

It's important to take care of yourself during this process. This process of picking up the pieces can take a long time.

Challenges of involuntary leaving

Being left is challenging for several reasons. Based on my personal experience of being left and kicked out, as well as experiences of the people I interviewed, below are some of the greatest challenges people faced and suggestions for how to deal with them. As psychiatrist Sandra from Rio de Janeiro said, "When you have to leave, you're not dealing with the anxious aspects of having to make a choice, but the depressive aspects of losing something. The first and most important loss is the loss of agency." Losing agency, or the feeling that we control our own actions, is a huge blow to our sense of self.[3] There are several aspects worth considering.

Shock and surprise. Being left or forced out often comes as a shock, as it did for Zenglo. Physically, our bodies may go into anxiety mode where our breathing becomes shallow, our heart starts to pound, thoughts race, and we start sweating. Unfortunately, this physical response often comes at an inopportune time, just when there is information we need to take in and understand. When you're blindsided like this, breathing is your friend. We can't intentionally stop our bodies sweating or our heart pounding, but we can control our breathing. Forcing ourselves to take deep, slow breaths can help slow down the other physiological symptoms and give us a bit more attention to focus on the matters at hand.

You often had no choice in the matter. So much of this book is about the power of choice to think carefully about making decisions that are right for you. With involuntary leaving, that all goes out of the window. While making an active decision is better than just letting things roll, when things that are out of your control happen, it is easy to focus on the lack of agency, the distress, and how out of control everything feels. Another more helpful approach is to focus instead on all the choices you are able to make now. I know that may seem like gallows humor. You may be saying sarcastically, "Yes, how wonderful that my spouse kicked me out. Now I get to make choices!"

I understand. It's not easy. Even so, it can be immensely powerful to shift the focus on what you are free to do. This includes making choices to ensure you are safe, to take care of yourself and your family, to find things to ground you and keep you focused on moving forward, one step at a time – *and to acknowledge these choices as demonstrating your agency and deliberately moving your life forward.* We all have unexpected things happen to us, that we didn't pick and probably didn't want. What's powerful is how we choose to react to events beyond our control.

One of the most spectacular examples of the power of choice in a seemingly powerless situation is in Viktor Frankl's book *Man's Search for Meaning.* [4] After an enormous amount of suffering in a concentration camp, Frankl describes the last human freedom that cannot be taken away as freedom to choose your attitude in any circumstances. He describes how these choices, such as his choice to remain at the camp to use his skills as a physician to help others, add deeper meaning to our lives.

It forces you to change in a way you might not have wanted to change. Many of us have moments of our lives in which we are on autopilot. We arrive at work not fully remembering our drive, or we make it through a day and wonder where the time went. Sometimes we have weeks or even years in which we may operate by routine. We may get to a place in our lives where we have enough money to cover our basic needs, a spouse or partner who's always there, and enough television, hobbies or friends to keep us going without us really needing to think about it. Then Bam! We get kicked out or left. Suddenly, everything is up in the air. We may be tempted to stomp our feet and shout. We didn't want to have to learn how to pick up the pieces, or how to be courageous, or how to ask for help (when we hate asking for help). We were fine the way we were, and if the other person hadn't felt that way, then we could stay in our safe bubble. Again, I understand these feelings very well.

I will duck as I write this, but what a wonderful opportunity to be shaken out of our complacency! While many people go into coasting mode in long-term relationships or in later life, being left or kicked out is a clear sign that there is more for us to learn. And as in any endeavor, we can do it grudgingly or we can do it cheerfully. We can pretend it doesn't need to get done and hide under the covers. Or we might as well grit our teeth and just get it done. If "cheerfully" is too much of a stretch, then maybe just "hopefully" or "with an open mind" is enough, or perhaps "with curiosity about how things will turn out." It's fine to allow ourselves a little time to stomp our feet and to be annoyed and upset that this happened. But then it's time to move onward with our lives.

It forces you to face the fact that things might not have been as good as you thought they were. When Clark told his wife he was leaving, his wife was shocked. He thought to himself, "Wow. If you didn't know I was unhappy and you didn't see this coming, that's why I'm leaving." Like Clark's wife, sometimes we feel blindsided at first, and then perhaps in retrospect we may consider that we *should have* seen it coming.

Other times, we are truly blindsided and could not have seen it coming — but that doesn't always stop us from obsessing over every detail to see if we can magically unravel the secret of how this happened. Likewise, in business, events can sometimes lead us to re-interpret the past, and sometimes to realize that we were indulging in wishful thinking, rather than reality.

The first order of business when we are kicked out or left is to ensure we are safe, we are stable, and that we have an immediate path forward. The 'how' and 'why' can wait until those necessities are taken care of. If they do keep intruding, it's okay to use a little healthy denial: you can tell yourself out loud, "I will think about that later" or you can picture yourself picking up the intrusive thoughts about 'how' and 'why' and placing them in a box in your head that you will deal with when you can.

You may feel unwanted, undeserving, unloved, or not good enough. For many of us, these feelings are hard enough to manage on a day-to-day basis, but if an important person in our life then leaves us, it can be a devastating blow. We may be plunged into despair because it feels like their decision reflects on us. It's hard not to take it personally. If your partner has fallen in love with someone else, or needs their freedom, or just doesn't want to cohabitate anymore, it can be very painful to accept that they are ready to move. You may be all too ready to blame yourself, and to look for ways in which you might have done things differently. It may help to think in terms of growing apart, rather than seeking to assign blame. Deeply hurtful though it is, it may simply be that your partner has outgrown the relationship. This doesn't mean there's anything wrong with you – just that your paths have diverged. Be gentle with yourself. These feelings will pass.

If you do feel that you were at fault, or that your behavior might have been less loving that it might have been, then you can take steps to address this. I find it helpful to consider the steps that Zen Master and spiritual teacher Thich Nhat Hanh[5] suggests, based on Buddha's teachings:

- Take responsibility for causing someone pain;
- Strive to understand the other person's suffering by listening deeply;
- Sincerely apologize; and
- Renew our resolve to act with compassion toward this person and toward everyone.

And I like to add: do all these things, and then *move on*. Even if you feel you were a bad partner, there's no need to punish yourself forever. Figure out how to make amends — some people find it helpful to write down a short account of what happened, or to make a list of their perceived shortcomings. Enlist the help of a qualified counselor, spiritual guide, or other mentor if necessary. The other party may not always accept your amends graciously, but that doesn't matter. They may come round in time, but meanwhile, you have done your best to make peace with the other person and with yourself. And try and accept that, even if you feel guilty, some of it was out of your control. Think about it. Will you ever know exactly what happened? Probably not. Will you be able to identify what you need to learn from the situation and then be able to move on? Absolutely. Relationships end, the lessons remain. Author Melody Beattie says that our mistakes are recyclable – we can learn from them, and apply our new knowledge next time around.[6] Meanwhile, indulge in some mindful self-care. Deep breathing, meditation, music, walking, and other exercise are all helpful. And don't forget the macaroni and cheese – and the mojitos!

You feel dumb that you didn't figure it out ahead of time. Or maybe you did know and just didn't want to accept it. We've all been there. Our inner voice is speaking, but we refuse to listen to it. How many times do we need our intuition to tell us, "I told you so" before we trust it? Of course, we could continue to feel dumb or to punish ourselves for our supposed lapses. Or we could identify what we need to learn from the situation using the above techniques and move on. Even if in retrospect, everything was crystal clear – like Clark's wife might have realized afterwards that it was obvious he was unhappy – we sometimes need to accept that we didn't see it then. Again, punish ourselves, or learn from it, pledge to do better, and move on? It's our choice.

There is a sense that the one who is left behind is deserving of pity or scorn. No one wants to appear as the rejected party, and we may worry what other people think of us. There's good news and bad news on this one. The bad news is that we can't control what other people think of us. The good news is that we can't control what other people think of us. So, we are under no obligation to try to change their minds. We can't anyway! No matter what happens to us in life, we can choose to carry ourselves with dignity. If someone wants to think you're a bad person because you were fired, there's not much you can do about it. Do *you* think you're a bad person? Do you want to walk around all day, every day, feeling ashamed and terrible? You can if you want to, but that doesn't sound like a good approach to me. I'm a big fan of mantras, as mentioned earlier, and mantras are a perfect fit for situations where we're left or kicked out.

Figure out what you want to say, simply, non-defensively, honestly, and directly, and then repeat as needed. So if someone says, "I'm so sorry to hear your wife left you," even if it feels like a punch in the gut, you can say, "Thank you. It's been challenging, and I'm glad we are moving on." And if they don't get the hint and follow up with, "You must feel awful, having her walk out on you like that!" You can hold your head high and say, "Thank you. It's been challenging, and I'm glad we are moving on." If for some reason they don't get it, a third time should do the trick. (If not, just shake your head and walk away.)

This can be effective you feel that your behavior was less than ideal as well. Decide on a "cover statement" that admits responsibility, but which also points a way forward. You see this in the media all the time: "I made some decisions that in retrospect were not wise, and I'm taking some time to spend with my family." I don't recommend this as an ideal step forward, but ideally you can take responsibility for your actions, and state what you need: space, time, support, or whatever it is you need. And you can work on learning from the situation and becoming a better person.

What to take away when leaving isn't your choice

Many people reported that involuntary leaving was hardest to process precisely because it wasn't their choice. I have found, though, that involuntary leaving forces us to grow in ways that are different from the process of choosing to leave. Here are some ideas on what you can take away when leaving is forced upon you.

You will be okay. We do not die when leaving is the choice of another, and not ours. Yes, there will be pain, and yes, your ego may be bruised, and yes, you will survive. Most likely, if my interviews are any guide, you will emerge stronger and with a better sense of yourself.

You have an opportunity to move forward and make changes to your life. Even when you don't choose your circumstances, you can always choose how you respond. Without in any way minimizing the pain of events, rejection can open new doors. Being fired opens us up to identifying what we'd like to do next. Being left by a partner gives us the chance to determine how we want to live our lives differently. Being ghosted by a friend means we can spend time on other aspects of our life that we may have been neglecting. Given that the situation was not in our control anyway, there may be utility in grieving and then identifying how to make lemonade out of these lemons.

Other people's opinions about the situation are not necessarily true and they often/nearly always don't matter. In fact, often they're false, or based on false assumptions or gossip or incomplete information.

There's a saying, "What other people think of me is none of my business."

In thinking about involuntary leaving, it was painful to realize that part of my pattern of leaving stems from — sometimes — being left first. I have had the experience where in a close relationship the other person withdraws to the point where it's a relationship in name only. And yet it continues. Sometimes there are protracted, painful discussions about "us." Sometimes there is no actual conversation although we both know that we are growing apart. Our relationship has become habit, a kind of comfort with the other person despite the challenges. The dread of ending things keeps the relationship running on fumes.

This isn't the easy way out. The tension builds and both parties maintain denial and refuse to talk about it for weeks, months, even years. Usually I'm the one who blinks first. I finally push the situation to the brink and say, "What are we doing here?" and "What do we want?" Then I'm usually the one to do the dirty work of the actual leaving, packing up my belongings, taking care of logistics, and having the difficult "goodbye" conversations. It's not a role I enjoy but it somehow seems better than the pressure of unresolved tension.

I have also had the experience of turning things around: of insisting we discuss the situation and then forging on ahead together. While writing this chapter, I realized that this kind of withdrawal by partners, friends and employers has happened to me a few times, leaving me to initiate confronting the issue. What was going on? I decided actively to explore this and tried to seek out old friends who had been left behind in my life. My friend Billy was exceptionally insightful. He and I were good friends in New York, and after I had a traumatic breakup and moved away, our friendship had faded somewhat. Billy was frank with me. He said, "Your independence is fierce. Some people really need to be needed, but you don't. You can sometimes be harsh when you make it clear that you don't need the other person. And some people don't get it when you say sincerely that you want to be with them, but you don't need them. I don't think it's conscious. I think it's just such a part of who you are that you don't realize you're doing it."

He went on, "I think it's the same with your employers. You make it clear – intentionally or not – that you can do things on your own and they withdraw. Then you feel abandoned and try to repair the relationship, but it's too late. And you don't want to be in that situation so you leave." I adore Billy, and I am so glad we've rekindled our friendship. I think he's right on.

Perhaps because my childhood has been full of leaving, I am independent, which as Billy pointed out, doesn't sit well with everyone. In addition, I think he's correct that sometimes I'm not as diplomatic about it as I could be. I've taken his words to heart and am thinking about how I can be more sensitive in these situations, as well as how I can better understand those who might not feel so fiercely independent and choose to stay.

Being left or kicked out can be extraordinarily challenging to our sense of self and how we see ourselves in the world. A single chapter can't do justice to the heartache, the self-doubt, the utter wreckage our lives can feel like. It is useful to consider the side of the equation of the ones who are left when we contemplate leaving. The ones we leave may experience the kind of pain, bewilderment, or shock discussed in this chapter. To me, this highlights how imperative it is to have frank and direct conversations with people, and to be kind as we take care of ourselves. We will never be able to eliminate pain from our lives as we make decisions about when to stay and when to leave, but we can do our best to reduce suffering through honesty, kindness, and compassion.

Chapter 11: Can You Ever Go Back?

Zenglo left China in 1988 when he was 25 years old, with $42 in his pocket, two suitcases, ramen noodles and a banana as a next meal, and an acceptance letter to attend graduate school in the U.S. He described his trip as "the first time I ever left my hometown, left China, first time on a plane, first time in the U.S."

He returned to China for the first time about ten years later. He told me:

I had very mixed emotions. I hadn't seen my parents for ten years. I was still single, but I had more than the $42 I left with. I went to see my parents and be back as a professional, which felt very good. I also wanted to resolve some of my old issues with the Chinese because when I left China in 1988, I felt resentful about wanting China to be a better country. When I went back, I decided to stay at the Beijing Friendship Hotel.

That hotel was very famous when I left China because it was only for foreigners. On the surface, there was a strong business reason to stay there, because it was only 15 minutes from my work. But the inside reason is I wanted to resolve my resentment. When I lived there, I had been blocked by the hotel because I was Chinese. That hotel is exclusively for foreigners, and it's a privilege to go in because of the foreigners there. I deliberately chose that hotel so I could get in. I think of it as my private revenge. I invited all my family there just to have dinner. It was so fancy. Probably eight waiters were there to take care of my family because I was now considered a foreigner.

Zenglo's experience made it clear that he never considered going back to the same China, but he definitely wanted to go back to visit, and to conduct that visit in a triumphant manner. He also went back as a "foreigner" despite staying 15 minutes from home and being around his family.

This chapter describes how we may or may not be able to ever go back. The prevailing thought in this chapter is philosopher Heraclitus's statement that, "No man ever steps in the same river twice, for it's not the same river and he's not the same man."

In my interviews, I found three types of "going back." First, quite a few of us went back temporarily to transition into leaving. A second option was people who went back to visit, often triumphantly, to remind themselves (and perhaps the ones they left) of how far they had come and why they left in the first place. And third were those who changed their minds and went back for good.

Few of those interviewed for this book did in fact wish to return on a permanent basis, but some made a go of it and were successful. We all have opportunities to stay and go, and there's no right or wrong way.

Going back during the transition
After summoning the courage to leave, many people found themselves going back to an ex off and on. Most of us were embarrassed about this, and saw it as neediness, in that we didn't

make a clean break. And yet, if making a break was easy, we would have already ended it, right?

---

*There was a lot of lingering after I left [my girlfriend of seven years]. After I moved out, I kept running back to her every time she called for a booty call. One day a friend of mine asked me what the hell I was doing. I said it feels good to be with her. She said, "Look yourself in the mirror and ask yourself what feels better: A quick 15 minute f*ck or your pride?" I ended it immediately. In that moment, I felt the freedom of letting go, the euphoria of finally being free. In that moment I literally went from being heartbroken and sometimes wanting her back to 'I'm done.'*

-Karen (Sydney)

I think making the trip (or trips) back during the transition is okay. In a way it's part of making sure that the decision is final, and it's also a part of the leaving process for some. Eventually, though, it's important to move on and either go back for good, leave for good, or transform the relationship. Otherwise, it's impossible to move on with your life to the next adventure.

Going back to visit
Zenglo's visit above was an example of wanting to return triumphant, and to him, it was a successful and happy visit that helped him banish many of the concerns he had about leaving China and helped him to integrate his experience into his life story.

Given my peripatetic childhood, I also went back to visit for a while. Between eight and 18 years old, I lived in four houses in suburban

Atlanta, which our family calls by their street names: Davis Road, Windsor Oaks, Oakrill Road, and Emerson Street. After high school and after I left for the Army, my parents moved again, so I didn't have a "home" to go back to, although we had only lived on Emerson Street for about four years.

I felt compelled when I returned to Atlanta, however, to go on what I fondly referred to as my "Tour of Homes." I would drive to each home, sit outside in the car, and reminisce. At Davis Road, we had foot races in the front yard, and I explored the creek in the neighbors' yard. At Windsor Oaks, the sapling we had planted when I was 11 had become a huge tree, and I could almost make out my initials I scratched in the concrete of the curb. When I was on my "Tour of Homes", one time I got lucky and there was an open house at the Oakrill Road house. I could still remember watching MTV world premieres in the living room, and there was still a patch on the wall where I busted it with my knee when I was 12 years old. At Emerson Street, I fondly remember sitting in the rocking chair on the porch after school, reading my best friend's letters after she moved away. The "Tour of Homes" felt like a compulsion of sorts. I felt compelled to take half a day and drive all over to visit each home, every time I visited, for years. It's as if I knew I could not go back, and yet I still tried to return. It was my way of connecting to the past, of bringing together all those disparate experiences of my childhood. Over the next ten years, each time I visited Atlanta, I did the tour. Eventually I stopped, mostly because I felt that I had my own home by then. I had bought a house by myself and it truly felt like my "home" so that I no longer needed to keep seeking my roots from that era.

When I return to places where I've lived, I always look up old friends and catch up, but I rarely go to old homes anymore. Visiting the old places at this point feels a little dreamlike, a little unreal. Recently I visited my friend Ninfa in Riverside, California. She has lived in the same house for more than 25 years. We met in 1995 during my three years in Riverside before I moved again. As we drove from our dinner location to her house, and then took a detour so she could show me her new workplace, I had the feeling of being in a dream. Everything was so familiar and yet so different. I remember the name of a road I used to take it all the time as a shortcut to somewhere, but where? And I knew, 20 years later, that we needed to get in the left lane when we rounded a particular curve, but I didn't remember why. I remembered everything in bits and pieces. I remembered the fun lady in my neighborhood I would work out with, but not her name. I remembered that Ninfa and I would meet at our favorite Mexican restaurant with the best tortillas, but not its location. I knew a mutual friend lived in this area, but not who it was. With Ninfa's help, the gaps in my memory started filling in and slowly my mental map expanded, but then it was time to leave again.

Going back for good

Scott from Connecticut introduced himself to me by telling me that Wendy is his first and second wife and that he is her first and third husband. They divorced after ten years, she married someone else, and then after that relationship ended, they remarried, 21 years to the day after they were first married. He said, "I have a natural resistance to change. I still wished her a happy anniversary on our anniversary every year, even when she was married to someone else, and we always stayed close for our daughters." He said that when they married each other again, it didn't feel so much like going back, but more like they never parted. Wendy describes her experience differently. She said she felt she had to leave the relationship the first time because she was dissatisfied. She felt she was being taken for granted and that she needed to be free. She agreed they remained friends while they were divorced so they could be good parents to their children. When the relationship with her second husband eroded, Scott was there. They kept seeing each other at events for their children, and eventually agreed they wanted to get back together.

Sometimes we can go back, if we have changed, or if the situation has changed. For example, Laura and Nick in Portland had been married about ten years when they decided to divorce. The marriage just wasn't working any more. They were starting to separate assets and she was looking for an apartment when he was involved in a terrible car accident. Months of rehabilitation in the local hospital, with Laura at his side, convinced both that their marriage was worth saving. Laura said, "I couldn't have stayed with Nick before, but he's a different person now. We're right for each other now in a way we weren't before." Deciding to stay, she said, has made her a stronger person and their relationship is much better.

I was friends with an ex for a while and then I finally had to end the friendship. We had dated for ten years. When we were dating, he was close with my family and friends, and that didn't change after we broke up. His new boyfriend became my father's business partner, and everything was intertwined. Eventually I made the decision that I couldn't be friends. I don't think everyone around me understood. After four years, I remember saying, "I need to get you out of my life, I have to do this for me." I just needed the space and I needed to recalibrate. Now we are friends again, but we're not so intertwined. I see him a few times a year but it's a very different relationship than when we were "friends" before. I had to quit that and rebuild myself and come back in a different way.

-Eric (New York)

In my travels, I have returned a few times. I moved back to Washington DC after 15 years away and became an administrator at the university where I had been a graduate student. I also moved back to New York City after five years away. I returned to a new workplace but the same neighborhood and some of the same friends. Both times, it was both new and not new. Returning to Washington didn't work out, despite my best efforts to stay there.

In a 1980 interview in Playboy,[1] John Lennon was asked why he thought it was impossible that the Beatles would ever reunite. His answer: *Do you want to go back to high school? Why should I go back ten years to provide an illusion for you that I know does not exist? It cannot exist.*

Some people say they can never go back.

I thought I could always go back to the job I loved in London, but now I know there's no place for me there. Either you change, your needs change, or the situation changes. When I left London, I was very sad because of the collection of people. But that moment is over.

-Melissa (New York)

Others described leaving as an important step in their journey, regardless of whether they ever went back. Sometimes it was important to leave so they could change and become a different person.

There's never a wrong choice. You can quit a job and come back. There's always something to learn in the meantime, but you can't make any mistakes. It's never back to Square 1 because there is no Square 1. We've aged already. It's not the same as it was. We change so much just by breaking up sometimes. Men go wild, and women find themselves, and then you can come back together and know what it's like to be with others.

-Rachel (Belgium)

If You Can't Leave

When people decide to stay, they usually conclude that the "cost" of leaving exceeds the benefits. Sometimes this is a rational calculation, and many times our emotional preferences and fears are also involved – just as they are in deciding to leave. When we work through the process indicated above, sometimes it doesn't matter what our pros and cons list says we should do: we just want to stay. As with leaving, we weigh things up, do some rational analysis and then make a decision based on intuition. To me, that's a feeling that needs to be respected and honored.

For people I interviewed, most frequently this decision came down to family. Many people indicated they planned to stay in their (unhappy) current living and work situations until their children finished high school, or because they were taking care of elderly or ill parents. Most people wanted to keep their children's lives generally stable and minimize moving; others had obligations and strong desires to stay close to family.

For example, when I interviewed AJ, he was deciding whether to leave his marriage. He knew his relationship with his wife was over, but he was highly concerned about the impact a separation would have on their four-year-old son. "I grew up with two parents, and I really had a great childhood," AJ said. "I want that for my son. I don't want to subject him to being shuttled back and forth between houses or having awkward moments when his mother and I both show up at school for him." AJ was also concerned about separating finances, moving out, and other logistical aspects of leaving. In the meantime, he stayed. "I figure it will become clear when I really need to leave," he said. "Otherwise, I will stay there and maintain a solid household for my son as long as I can."

For others, more intangible aspects compel us to stay. Prea said that she delayed leaving a job she disliked for several years. A senior colleague kept urging her to stay, even though he was unhappy himself, because he wanted to continue to work with her. Prea said, "I stayed too long because I was concerned about my reputation, my status, money ... I also had a fear of being alone and of disappointing my colleagues by leaving." She said the process of ultimately leaving that job, "required understanding the beliefs I let run me. We are all in our own way seeking to be seen and heard and appreciated and loved." She has since directly addressed the fear and insecurity she felt led her to stay at an unhappy job through meditation and therapy.

Others decide they no longer want to keep leaving and choose intentionally to stay and face their fears. As indicated above, Billy from Louisiana described how he made a choice to stay. He and his partner, Robert, had been arguing frequently, and Billy thought they were about to break up. "I decided that if I left him, I'd have to go through all this stuff with another person and go through the same thing I'm going through now. I thought to myself, 'Instead of going through all that again, I'm going to clean this mess up right now.' I've stayed with him ever since."

Wanting to leave but deciding to stay doesn't mean we have to be unhappy. People who decided to stay offered suggestions for how to stay with grace.

Clarify our thinking. Like AJ and Prea, sometimes we need to stay for a while or for a long time for reasons we deem more important than the reasons we need to leave. We can feel better about deciding to stay if we are clear in our own minds about why. Rather than thinking, "I have to stay and I'm stuck," we can think, "I'm choosing to stay because I want my daughter to finish high school here." It doesn't change the situation, but we can feel better about it.

Change what we can. If we feel stuck in our job and our home and our routines, it may be possible to change something that shakes us up enough to feel better without needing to upend everything in our lives. Applying for a different job at the same organization, or getting a pet, or starting a new hobby can help us continue moving forward in our lives even when one part needs to stay the same.

Take a break. A vacation, a working vacation, or even a weekend away from our routine can help us feel better and give us an opportunity to think of our lives differently. Life doesn't stop just because we can't leave.

Start planning. If we can't leave now but can leave in a specified amount of time (such as when our children finish school), start dreaming now. Enjoy the process of making plans. We can save money, consider how we want to live in the future, or explore new opportunities so that when we can leave, we'll be ready.

Keep learning and growing. Alma from Washington DC said that she hopes to move up to a more senior job once her son graduates from high school. "Until then, I'm learning as much as I can," she said. She takes joy in seeing her son with his friends and sports teams. She feels confident she and her husband are making the right decision.

Chapter 12: On Leaving and Staying

As people all over the world continue the leaving revolution and seek better lives, as a leaver, I know I will never know the quiet comfort of having lived in a neighborhood all my life or celebrating a 25th wedding anniversary. I believe my life is richer because of my choices, but I have lived in the (more or less) four corners of the US (Florida, Southern California, Oregon, New York City) and in Europe. I have carried my childhood stuffed bear George with me in a box around the world and across the country for 30 years. I have met many people and explored many neighborhoods. I'm a packing and transitioning pro.

As I have pondered leaving and staying, I have realized how wrong I was in some ways. When I started research for this book, I conceived of it as a celebration of leaving, because that was my experience. I had the courage to leave, I am good at leaving, and I have an integrated sense of being a leaver. I initially thought staying was for suckers! Why would anyone stay? How wrong I was. First, I'm not quite the leaver I thought I was. Second, there's strength and courage in both leaving and staying. The strength is not in whether you leave or stay, but in making a decision that is right for you and true to your soul's purpose.

I am certainly well familiar with the old adage: "You can't change deck chairs on the Titanic." But you know what I always think when I hear that adage? THERE WERE SOME PEOPLE ON THE TITANIC WHO SURVIVED. ... Which means: Sometimes there IS a better place for you to be, geographically, than where you are right now. ... I truly believe this. Sometimes running away really, really, really does work.

-Author Elizabeth Gilbert, as posted on Facebook[1]

Initially, I felt that I was an expert in leaving. My experiences certainly supported that belief. In my mind, leavers are bold, decisive, action-oriented, independent and assertive. I saw stayers as passive, wishy-washy, dependent and unassertive. In interviewing more than 100 people about leaving, however, I heard fantastic stories of leaving – and wonderful stories of staying. I heard from people who considered leaving but who ultimately stuck it out and are stronger for it. I heard from people who thought they were leaving, but who actually became more focused on the leaving itself rather than on what was right for them.

As I reviewed how I left home, left partners, left jobs, left neighborhoods, even left friends, I saw that sometimes my leaving fit the pattern I had assumed – I left for opportunity, for adventure, for fun. Sometimes, however, I left a situation because the relationships there had had become intolerable. And in some cases, I left when it was clear that the relationship was already over. In essence, I left physically because the other person had already checked out emotionally. This has happened with partners, friends, and jobs. Realizing that sometimes I did the official wrap-up of an already-dead relationship made me think differently about my identity as a leaver, and about leaving and staying generally.

I always follow my gut. If it feels right, then I do it. There will be so many things going on in your head when you're thinking of leaving. Don't listen to your head. Listen to your gut. You can't go wrong.

-Petra (Sweden)

I also came to realize that part of my own leaving story is that sometimes I physically left a situation because other people had actually left me first. My leaving was in reaction to a departure that had already taken place.

My family wasn't present for me. They essentially abandoned me, so I had to leave home. My husband changed his mind about what he wanted, from initially wanting to be an urban trial lawyer, to wanting to raise kids in a rural area with the kind of childhood he had. He had every right to change his mind, but mine didn't change. I didn't want to have kids then and the timing wasn't right for what I wanted out of life. That's when I left. I left a partner after she cheated on me and lied to me about it. But she really "left" me first.

I left jobs because I wanted to move on. In each of these decisions, my employer first left me: by choosing not to protect their employees from harassment, by making it clear they did not value or appreciate their employees, or by making it clear that their employees were there to do the grunt work and stroke their egos rather than to create a positive learning environment for everyone. It became clear that I did not have backup, support or advancement opportunities for me to stay.

Choosing yourself is SO important. People will leave you. You can leave them. As I'm still learning about what it is like to stay, I've identified a few ways to make staying more likely. I'm growing roots in my community. Greeting my neighbors, chatting with the grocers and dry cleaners, joining clubs, and truly integrating myself with my neighborhood. Second, I'm traveling a LOT. Mostly overseas, but I'm definitely getting out of the house and seeing new parts of the world – and at the same time, making sure to enjoy returning home. It's all very exciting. Finally, I'm building closer friendships. Some people I've known for a few years, and others are new. But by spending more time and energy on my friends instead of work, it makes more likely to stay instead of moving again. Finally, clarity of purpose is no joke. Knowing why I move and why I stay both will be helpful toward understanding this pattern.

Are you a stayer or a leaver?
Almost every person I spoke with was able to say immediately and with confidence whether they were a stayer or leaver. I heard over and over again, "Oh, I'm definitely a stayer," or "I'm a leaver." Most were consistent. They would stay in all areas of their life, including relationships, employment, living situation, and friends, or they would leave in all those areas. This makes sense because often changing one of these will result in changing others, such as when you move to a new city for a job.

I considered creating a scale of, "How you know you're a leaver or stayer," but then it seemed so obvious to most people that a scale probably isn't necessary. Instead, I did more research into the question, and the same themes came up.

Restlessness. Most leavers described a recurring sense of restlessness that they have experienced for most of their lives. At some point in a relationship, in a home, or in a job, they start to feel restless and to think about what else is out there, and how to have more excitement and adventure. It doesn't mean they would always act on this restlessness, but they would typically identify it as a need to do something different, whether it's go travel for a little bit, paint the apartment, start a new hobby, or sometimes leave something. Some of us have felt that this restlessness is a character flaw and that it's more "mature" to be a stayer. Others have embraced our restlessness and enjoyed a life of adventure.

Comfort with not knowing. Overall, leavers tend to be more comfortable with not knowing what will happen next. Leavers seem to be more curious about what will happen instead of being anxious it will turn out differently than they expect. Similarly, comfort with not knowing means that leavers tend to be more comfortable with change. Perhaps this comfort comes from knowing that if leavers don't like the change, they could always leave, whereas stayers feel they will need to hang in there and make it work out.

Views of relationships as permanent vs. temporary. Stayers tended to view relationships as permanent. "Once we're friends, we're friends for life." Stayers work hard to keep friendships, sometimes even if it may not be to their benefit, and are quite distressed when people move on. They are loyal and consistent friends. Leavers, on the other hand, tend to subscribe to the view that people come and go in our lives — and that's okay. Generally, leavers don't try as hard to keep friends, and generally set the bar at letting a friend go much lower than do stayers. Not that leavers don't have loyalty or commitment or long-term relationships; they do. They just see relationships differently.

So, do you think of yourself as a leaver or stayer? And how much difference does it make to your life? Maybe not that much in the long run. It could, however, lead to thinking differently about how you approach situations: is your tendency to leave or stay? Do you feel restlessness is wrong or an interesting part of who we are that leads us to explore something new? How do you view relationships with others?

We can learn from leavers and stayers

I now see leaving and staying as being about who we are and about where we choose to be in the world. I admire that leavers get to explore, have adventures, see new things, and follow their curiosity. They also don't accept bad behavior from anyone (or at least not for long). Leavers set a boundary and draw a line. The motto of leavers is, "Don't mess with me," with the implied threat of "(or I'll walk away)." Perhaps leavers have the same biological instincts as songbirds, who even when captive develop a restlessness to fly through the night during migration season. Leavers also tend to be very focused on what's next, what's coming up.

Of course, there are plenty of downsides to being a leaver. It's hard to get close to people when you're always ready to walk away (or run!) It's tough to have a relationship with someone when you're feeling defensive, and your dukes are up. It takes a lot of energy to move or change jobs over and over. It's difficult to benefit from the work you did to transition into a place when you leave again soon after. In some cases, you keep facing the same issues repeatedly.

I realize that because I moved around so much as a kid, I was very casual about relationships coming and going in my life. I don't have people who have known me a long time other than family, and that's sometimes been challenging. When I meet new friends, I can fake it for a while, and many times I leave before they really get to know me. I know that I have this tendency to create friendships that are not deep and enduring. I don't open up and trust people and bring them into my life much, so I am not able to tell anyone, "I'm hurting in my relationship." I've aone so much work on building relationships. Now I require for myself and for whoever I'm dating that we each have best friends and a strong circle of friends. I know I have to have an outlet and I have to set up these parameters to ensure my partner has an outlet too.

-Clark (New York City)

Stayers, though, may be more likely to enjoy the permanence of where they are. They don't keep an eye on the horizon, always scanning for what's next. If they travel, they always go home again. Even stayers who aspire to be bigger, better, or faster may temper those desires if it takes them away from their home. They are content. They don't feel the itch to hit the road, other than taking an occasional vacation, but if they do feel like leaving, it can be massaged away or allowed to fade.

I'm a stayer. I've been pretty consistent my whole life, but it feels like it's boring to say that. I haven't really changed jobs – I've been a registered nurse for almost 36 years. I haven't moved. I have had a very solid family. I have real staying power! I think it's in my genes to be who I am in terms of being responsible, staying put, and being reliable. It may be boring, but I'm comfortable. It's easy. Change is hard. Leaving is hard. I'm thinking about changing my job but haven't been brave enough to do it yet. I was thinking that if I leave, it has to be for a really deep reason.

-Deb (Connecticut)

This is a lovely picture of solid contentment, but sadly it doesn't work in every situation. Think of a workplace that employed only stayers. Pretty stagnant, right? If everyone stayed, there would be few truly original ideas. If people left only when they retired, the business would quickly go under.

Now think of a workplace (or a society) of leavers. What chaos! If everyone is leaving all the time, there's hardly a sense of continuity, of process. Few projects would ever be completed, and it would be difficult to manage so much change all the time. Most workplaces have a mix of those who stay and those who move around. It's good to have that mix.

And like workplaces, it's refreshing and exciting that there are both leavers and stayers in the world. We each bring our unique strengths, and we influence each other. I've been inspired by others choosing to make the leap to entrepreneurship, or another job or adventure. And others have told me that my courage to leave a romantic relationship, job, or any situation that wasn't working for me, made them think hard about what they wanted, and to make changes to ensure they were both happy and satisfied.

We each have a lot to learn from each other. Leavers can learn to tolerate a bad situation a little longer to understand the good in that perseverance. To push themselves to be a little more creative to find a twist or a hack to make a bad situation more tolerable. To squeeze every last drop of learning from a situation before leaving. To be satisfied in what we have. To find joy in everyday life, to slow down, appreciate, enjoy, celebrate each day instead of focusing on the horizon and always thinking about what's next. To understand that staying isn't necessarily a lack of strength or courage.

I get why there are unhappy people who won't leave. I was unhappy in a relationship for four years, and I wonder how long it would have dragged on if I hadn't been given a nudge. I never think unhappy stayers are complicit in the situation. It could be they're scared to leave, they're comfortable enough, the job pays my bills, the job market sucks, or we have kids together. When I was 27, one of my really close friends was murdered by her boyfriend because she tried to leave. She wasn't staying out of laziness or complacency – she was staying because she was terrified. When she finally grew the tenacity and courage to say, 'I want to leave you,' he killed her. She was a person who taught me to never judge someone for staying in a situation that looks unhappy. They may be unhappy but at least they have control of the situation. It's dangerous to say you need

*to just get brave and leave or grow a spine and leave. It's
not that simple.*

-Karen (Sydney)

Stayers can learn from leavers to have those difficult conversations
where we stand up for ourselves and say we're not going to put up
with poor treatment any more. To have the courage to shake up your
life when things aren't working. To pay more attention to what makes
you happy and a little less to what others want. To take wild chances
and develop our confidence so we know we're able to land anywhere
on our feet and keep going.

It's important to make individual choices that work for us, and always
to strive for what serves the greatest good. Of course, we can't know
other people's thoughts and fears and circumstances, so I'm learning
not to judge what I can't fully know. In this as in all things, we must
make our own way through life.

Can we change our spots?
The U.S. was founded on leaving. Most Americans have at least some
family members who left their home countries to emigrate to the U.S.
We are a country of immigrants. We move more often than most
others, we leave jobs, we get divorced, we move on in our lives as a
culture. It's all about moving, going, leaving. Little wonder we're
reclaiming our roots as leavers.

In *Travels with Charley in Search of America*, John Steinbeck
captured a sense of North Americans as leavers as he told
his neighbors about his upcoming road trip.[2]

I saw in [my neighbors'] eyes something I was to see over and over in every part of the nation – a burning desire to go, to move, to get under way, anyplace, away from any Here. They spoke quietly of how they wanted to go someday, to move about, free and unanchored, not toward something but away from something. I saw this look and heard this yearning everywhere in every state I visited. Nearly every American hungers to move.

As someone who's moved many times, it's easy to feel that I don't belong anywhere, that I have no "home." In fact, unlike many of my age-peers, I do not have a "family home." Neither my parents nor grandparents have a family home to which I return at holidays. Everything that is mine is in the house or apartment where I live. There are no family heirlooms, or furniture that I grew up with that my parents still own. But rather than feeling that I don't belong anywhere, I have decided that I am a person of the world, and that I belong *everywhere*. Wherever I am becomes my home.

I started writing this book, as I saw it, to explain leaving to those stayers out there. I was proud of my leaving, of choosing deliberately, repeatedly, to leave situations that were not working for me and to be brave and bold enough to find situations that did work for me. I'm also a bit defensive about leaving: when other people talk about their family home, or their mother keeping their childhood bedroom the same, or about their long-term relationships, none of which I have, I feel like I need to put up my dukes and say with an edge to my voice that I made decisions that work for me and no one should question me.

Along the way, something strange happened. I started longing to learn what it is like to stay. I started wondering how people could stay in marriages in circumstances where I would have been gone, such as when a spouse cheats. Or when at work, when I would have left, such as in the case of a colleague who got demoted after being a whistleblower, but who chose to stay. Choosing to pass on a great job opportunity across the country because you're highly invested in your community or your family nearby. All of this in the context of the current leaving revolution.

Is it really possible for a leaver to become a stayer, or vice versa? I think stayers can be compelled to leave should the situation worsen significantly. And I think leavers can learn to stay. Much of this book encourages stayers to think about leaving, or helps leavers to leave in ways that are smoother and more positive. Could a leaver like me ever become a stayer? I'm not sure, but I'm interested in trying it out.

Here is what I've learned from a lifetime of leaving. These are my approaches to the world, refined though the lens of leaving and staying – my own, and perspectives from people I interviewed for this book.

So how do you choose to live? Do you choose to live in a state of unhappiness, exhaustion, and futility … or do you choose to live with a sense of excitement and possibility about all the uncertainty in our lives?

-Author Susan Jeffers in *Feel the Fear and Do It Anyway*[3]

Do what you have to do
I think this is a key component of having the courage to make your own path. And yet when I've talked with people who have made bold changes in their lives – moving away, leaving a partner, job, or religion – they don't really describe their paths in terms of courage. When I say, "Wow! That was brave," they typically shrug. To a one, they describe what their

leaving and their choices not as brave, but as *what they had to do*. To a one, they say, "It was just what I had to do." I still think there is bravery in this. There is bravery in saying, "This is my life, and I choose to live it in the way I want," whether that involves leaving or staying, kids or no kids, travel or no travel. As Karen from Sydney said, "I never understood why my friends called me brave. It takes courage to think you're doing a crazy thing and do it anyway.'"

I am strong. My life's work is managing these challenges, succeeding despite my tendency to choose the most difficult path possible. Focused on improvement, lifting as I climb. I am trying to enjoy the adventure, even as I gnaw my own arm off sometimes to be free.

Be kind

I've learned that when leaving, it's important to be kind. This may seem obvious, but in talking with people who leave and people who are left, we each have our unique experiences and processes that affect how we understand someone leaving us. When I leave, it's become easier for me to manage my own emotional and logistical aspects of leaving: making the decision to leave is easier, and I no longer must hit rock bottom before I leave (as Eric discussed, above). Those difficult conversations aren't as stressful as they used to be, and I've become a pro at logistics. This has resulted in me having more space and energy to see others' perspectives of what the experience is like. In leaving partners and jobs and homes, I've made plenty of bad mistakes – especially hurting people's feelings when I needn't have, which is what I regret the most. As I interviewed brave leavers and brave stayers, I've expanded my concept of what leaving is like for others and have increased my compassion for everyone involved. As John Watson said, "Be kind, for everyone you meet is fighting a hard battle."[4]

Leaving brings with it difficult conversations. It means saying goodbye. There are also the awkward conversations with others later about why you made the decisions you did. For example, "You two were so good together — why did you break up?" or, "Why would you want to move to [new city]?" or, "Why would you leave school?" How do you manage these conversations? You manage them as you would the rest of the process: honestly, diplomatically, pleasantly, and forthrightly (and if you're a nerd like me, you make a list of potential responses). As I'm deciding what's right for me, it's good to see if it's possible to ease others' lives in the process.

Take chances; life is what you make it
Thinking through this process of leaving or staying is also a way of claiming our own power. The choice to take time to focus on what we really want and then to take steps to make it happen is enormously empowering. Leaving autopilot is scary, and exciting, and empowering. Of course, this process involves taking chances, and being brave. I agree with Andre Gide that you can't discover new oceans unless you have the courage to lose sight of the shore.[5] Not a single person I interviewed said they wished they hadn't taken a chance on leaving or staying. In fact, people I interviewed who were under 40 typically talked about the challenges of taking chances, including fear, logistics and consequences. Those over 50 typically volunteered that they wished they had taken more chances generally in their lives and said their fears were overblown.

I did things I did not understand for reasons I could not begin to explain just to be in motion, to be trying to ao something, change something in a world I wanted desperately to make over but could not imagine for myself.

-Author Dorothy Allison[6]

Sometimes we have to have a lot of experiences to understand what we want our lives to be. Changing our living situation, friendships, job, religion, even our hairstyle can help us identify what we like. This exploration part is what makes me feel so alive. Everyone who loves me knows I must be free and go on my adventures, and they know it doesn't mean I love them any less. And I hope that I can be that supportive, accepting, and understanding of my loved ones – that we all get to choose how we want to live our lives, and we do our very best to make the most of it. Life is too short to be unhappy. Rodrigo told me that his family in Sao Paulo, Brazil, has a tradition. At funerals, they are not sad. They say to each other that the deceased "led a well-lived life" and describe the person's adventures, chances taken and joys. I love that.

Leavers know they're leavers, but stayers don't always know they're stayers. I think many stayers have leavers inside, and if it wasn't for the fear, they would do it. I think it's more romantic to be a leaver. The idea of going where the weather fits your clothes is romantic to me. I grew up on stories of kids having amazing adventures with just a bag and a few necessities and that one special talisman that went with them everywhere. I have loved that idea since I was a kid.

-Katrina (New York)

Be grateful

I am so incredibly grateful to the people I have met along this journey. People encouraged me to stay and try a different way to succeed, people who confirmed that they also believed it was time for me to go, people who were excited for my new adventures when I left. They taught me how to make difficult decisions, how to have hard conversations, how to choose my life over what others want.

I met Michelle in Portland early in my academic career when she agreed to mentor me. She was so helpful to me during our first lunch meeting, and I thanked her profusely. She looked at me oddly after my third round of "Thank you SO very much." She thought for a moment, then said, "You can just say 'thank you' once. This is the kind of mentoring junior faculty deserve and what you all should be receiving. I'm not doing you a favor, I'm doing what I'm supposed to be doing." Wow. There is such a dearth of good mentoring, and she really hit the nail on the head.

My friend Phil in Washington DC, a stayer who has been at the same institution for more than 20 years, also gave me a life-changing approach that I carry with me to this day. Some years ago, I was complaining to Phil about my job. I felt that my boss was not supportive of my efforts to advance, there was an ongoing harassment investigation among my peers that was a bad situation, and I was getting mixed messages from my boss' director about my work. Phil listened as I gave him my litany of, "And this! And another thing! And this other thing too!" Finally he said quietly and with compassion, "Jen, how many red flags do you need?"

Boom.

The most important impact of gratitude to me is increasing compassion. The more I hear from people I've ruthlessly sought out as mentors and friends, the more I understand that most of us haven't had someone looking out for us, opening doors, and providing advice and feedback that is sometimes difficult to hear. When I think about that, I feel enormous gratitude toward those who took time for me, and I feel it's imperative on me to be that mentor for others. And when people ask me for assistance and then they are overly grateful, I use Michelle's words and say, "This is what you deserve." When they ask how they can repay me, I say, "All I ask is that you pass it on to others." That's one of the ways I express my gratitude.

Belonging means connections to both people and places.

Living in Portland, Oregon, was my first experience of waking up every day and thinking "I absolutely LOVE it here!" It made me wonder (simplistically) why people chose to live anywhere that didn't thrill them. It was very difficult to leave Oregon, but I always have a special place in my heart for Portland as one of my favorite places on the planet. And returning to New York City and my friends brought me joy I never thought possible about the continuity of friendships that have persisted through ups and downs and over the years. I still get a thrill when I see the Empire State Building or the Brooklyn Bridge. Over and over, I find that it's all about relationships AND it's also about place. It's about feeling connected to other people, and to the earth, or to your apartment or house, or to a routine. About feeling you matter, about feeling a part of something bigger than yourself, that outlasts our brief time here on earth.

In my leaving, especially leaving jobs and moving across the country, I have been yearning for a perfect balance of being a part of something larger, without feeling constricted by the tentacles of those relationships. Even the way I talk about relationships expresses how I see them: nurturing, strengthening, yet restrictive. I am slowly learning what I think stayers instinctively know: the joy of the connection is sometimes not despite the constrictions, but because of them.

In my leaving bravado, I make my decisions, express my agency, choose my own adventure. Then relationships and loss and longing creep up on me. Before I have realized it, I am in bed with them again, snuggling together as we huddle against the storms outside, safe hand in hand until I feel they've latched on and are draining my energy. I rip my life apart, change geography, change job, change my whole life. I feel the angst and terror of annihilation, I overcome it, and then loss and longing creep in again. Of course, it would be less expensive to deal with these fears head on instead of moving across the country, but they are sneaky. I confront them, I fight them, but they slip away into my peripheral vision. I know they're there. I spend weeks and months getting settled in my new home, developing new routines, refusing to pay attention, distracting myself, and denying the existence of these fears. I scramble back up and confront them again. Writing this book has been part of my journey to vanquish my own fears, and to help others learn in the process.

Challenges are worth it
As I think back over the eight schools I attended before I graduated high school, and the 27 places I've lived, I've made and lost a lot of friends. I love having friends around the country and around the world from my many moves and my travels. But that's not always useful when you need some help moving a couch, or a shoulder to cry on, or someone with whom to share good news. Because I've moved around so frequently, I've learned to separate the true gems of friendship from those friends who come and go in my life. This has been largely due to my experiences of leaving and being challenged to maintain friendships or let them go gracefully (or sometimes, not so gracefully).

I think of how many times I've sat in a room full of boxes and faced the seemingly impossible task of getting ready to start work on Monday, and I'm proud of my work ethic. I think of packing up and moving from New York City to Washington, D.C., two days after Hurricane Sandy hit, and I'm proud of my strength and fortitude. My skills in navigating systems and bureaucracies have been enormously strengthened by my challenges learning new workplace organizational structures and politics over and over and over again. Approaching difficult conversations about leaving – and being left – have greatly increased my compassion for others. Contemplating repeatedly whether to leave or stay has led me to develop a very clear picture of how I want to live and the kind of person I want to be. A key word in all this is resilience.

Psychologists define resilience as the process of adapting when faced with adversity, trauma, tragedy, threats, family problems, health issues, or work stress. Being resilient doesn't mean you don't experience stress; it only means that you are able to "bounce back," including by taking care of your stress and health, continuing to move toward your goals, maintaining perspective, staying hopeful, learning from your experiences, and seeking help when needed.

Leaving [my home country] has opened the door to everything. I've become so much open minded to the world. Not social issues, but cultures I didn't know existed, religions that would have baffled me before, ways of life and ways of learning. It's one of the best decisions I ever made.

-Karen (Sydney)

There's such value in working through the hard questions in our lives. How much of leaving is seeking happiness or contentment that feels impossible to achieve where you are? And how much of staying is choosing to find that happiness and contentment, or to live without it. How much of leaving is courage and how much of staying is fear? And vice versa?

Many leavers I talked to described the struggles of building relationships, as well as their significant strengths in learning to feel comfortable anywhere, being open to change, and being flexible. Stayers have had different challenges and different lessons. They reported being proud of being a source of consistency for many leavers, being able to find the good in any situation, and having great patience along with the hope that all difficult situations will pass. Everyone I talked to said their path was worth it, that the challenges were worth it. Many of us still struggle with some aspect of leaving or staying, and probably will for the rest of our lives. But I was struck by how hopeful and positive both the leavers and stayers I interviewed were. How they all — leavers and stayers — were glad for their paths, despite the challenges.

Your choices inspire others

The bravery to make a choice to live our lives, whether others agree or not, whether we succeed or fail, and whether we stay or leave, can be inspiring to others. I wrote this book to encourage people to take charge of their lives by considering carefully if they want to leave or stay. The courage comes in making a choice, regardless of what that choice is, and, as Henry David Thoreau said, going "confidently in the direction of your dreams."[7]

I have had extraordinarily close friends, women and men I've known for years and whom I've told everything. I've also had a few friendships go bust when we attempted to mix work with friendship. And of course, there are people with whom I just didn't "click." I have learned so much from friends, jobs, changes in how I see myself, changes in living situation, partners … I've had an enormous adventure traveling, meeting new people, becoming a cardboard box/house-packing expert. I've experienced the sadness of leaving, the guilt and shame of leaving, the joy of leaving for a new adventure (and to me, they're all adventures).

I am by no means perfect, and I've not always been as kind as I would like to have been. By and large, though, I think I've done well. For whatever reason, my temperament, upbringing, and circumstances conspired to make me a leaver. I am proud of my choices, and yet, every choice has the other side of the coin. I have lived all over the country. I've remodeled hundred-year-old houses on both east and west coasts. I've surfed on three continents (so far). I've traveled around the world and lived life on my terms. And yet … I will never celebrate a 50th wedding anniversary. I don't know what it's like to have a family home to go back to for years and years. Or to have kids and grandkids. I'm okay with that.

I hear friends and family members complain about friends or bosses or spouses who treat them poorly or take advantage of them, and I honestly no longer relate because I will no longer stay with someone who treats anyone like that. Those friendships are sometimes hard to let go of, especially because of the previous trust and intimacy that feels doubly violated by inconsiderate, rude, or plain mean behavior. And dear friends like Phil, with his expectations for friends that they are reasonable, considerate, fair, and honest, have further reinforced that sometimes it's better to be alone than to be with people who don't treat us well.

I think of myself as a leaver: I have left a profession, a city, two spouses ... and now I choose to stay in São Paulo. I want to be here because after a lot of hard work to get here, I now have the life I want: my parents and in-laws are here, friends, a good job, my wife's weekend house on the beach and mine in the mountains. I can travel as much as I want, and I really love my life. So I stay and work in São Paulo, and I'm free to do and be anything I want.

-Ricardo (Brazil)

We have so many choices, including whether to leave, change, or stay. As we all are creating a revolution of leaving, I am delighted that we are making choices to no longer merely tolerate what is no longer serving us. Whatever you decide to do – to leave or stay – be courageous, and have no doubt that you will make the right decision.

For Further Reading

Mythological and Theoretical Approaches to Leaving

- Ronald L. Grimes. (2002). *Deeply into the Bone: Re-inventing Rites of Passage.* University of California Press.
- Carl Jung. (1961). *Memories, Dreams, Reflections.* Vintage.
- Claude Levi-Strauss. (1995). *Myth and Meaning.* Schocken.
- Arnold Van Gennep. (1961). *Rites of Passage.* University of Chicago Press.

Leaving a Job or Career

- Marilyn J. Abraham. (2011). *First We Quit Our Jobs: How One Work Driven Couple Got on the Road to a New Life.* Dell.
- James Altucher. (2013). *Choose Yourself.* CreateSpace Independent Publishing Platform.
- Jeanne Boschert. (2015). *The Ethical Exit: Transition your Work and Love your Life.* Difference Press.
- Tim Ferris. (2009). *The Four-Hour Work Week.* Harmony.
- Herminia Ibarra. (2004). *Working Identities.* Harvard Business School Press.
- Pamela Slim. (2009). *Escape from Cubicle Nation.* Berkley.
- Marcea Weiss. (2008). *Leaving the Military: Your Deployment Guide to Corporate America.* Calypso.

Leaving a Spouse or Partner

- Ashton Applewhite. (1997). *Cutting Loose: Why Women Who End their Marriages Do So Well.* Harper Collins.
- Ramani Durvasula. (2015). *Should I Stay or Should I Go? Surviving a Relationship with a Narcissist.* Post Hill Press.
- Mira Kirshenbaum. (1996). *Too Good to Leave, Too Bad to Stay: A Step-by-Step Guide to Help You Decide Whether to Stay In or Get Out of Your Relationship.* Penguin Group.
- Amber Coverdale Sumrall. (1994). *Breaking Up is Hard to Do: Stories by Women.* Crossing Press.

- Jude Walsh. (2018). *Post-Divorce Bliss: Ending Us and Finding Me*. Difference Press.

Leaving Friends
- Jenny Offill and Elissa Schappell (Editors). (2007). *The Friend Who Got Away: Twenty Women's True Life Tales of Friendships that Blew Up, Burned Out or Faded Away*. Broadway Books.
- Jessica Smock and Stephanie Sprenger (Editors). (2014). *My Other Ex: Women's True Stories of Losing and Leaving Friends*. HerStories Project Press.

Leaving for Adventure
- William Finnegan. (2015). *Barbarian Days: A Surfing Life*. Penguin Books.
- Elizabeth Gilbert. (2007). *Eat, Pray, Love*. Riverhead Books.
- John Steinbeck. (1961/1997). *Travels with Charley in Search of America*. Penguin.
- Cheryl Strayed. (2013). *Wild*. Random House.

Leaving Home
- Sari Botton (Editor). (2014). *Never Can Say Goodbye. Writers on their Unshakable Love for New York*. Simon and Schuster.
- David Celani. (2011). *Leaving Home: The Art of Separating from Your Difficult Family*. Columbia University Press.
- Denise Zorer, Diana Polus, and Jennifer Wisdom. (2021). *Generation Z Guide to Leaving Home*. Winding Pathway Books.
- Hazel Rochman and Darlene Z. McCampbell (Editors). (1998). *Leaving Home: Stories*. HarperTeen.

Leaving a Religion
- Martha Beck.(2006). *Leaving the Saints: How I Lost the Mormons and Found My Faith*. Broadway Books.
- William Lobdell. (2009). *Losing My Religion: How I Lost My Faith Reporting on Religion in America – and Found Unexpected Peace*. Harper.

- Marlene Winell. (2013). *Leaving the Fold: A Guide for Former Fundamentalists and Others Leaving Their Religion*. Apocryphile Press.
- Rachel Held Evans. (2015). *Search for Sunday: Loving, Leaving, and Finding the Church*. Thomas Nelson.
- Barbara Brown Taylor. (2009). *Leaving Church: A Memoir of Faith*. HarperOne.

General Life Change

- Seth Godin. (2007). *The Dip: A Little Book That Teaches You When to Quit (and When to Stick)*. Portfolio.
- Kristina Hallett. (2018). *Own Best Friend*. Morgan James Publishing.
- James Hollis. (2005). *Finding Meaning in the Second Half of Life*. Avery.
- James Hollis. (2009). *What Matters Most*. Avery.
- Susan Jeffers. (1987). *Feel the Fear and Do It Anyway*. Jeffers Press.
- Susan Jeffers. (2004). *Embracing Uncertainty*. St. Martin's Griffin.

References

Chapter 1

[1] A new collection published in 2018 by the Joseph Campbell Foundation gathers Joseph Campbell's collected works in 18 books. These include *The Power of Myth, The Hero with a Thousand Faces, Myths to Live By*, and *The Hero's Journey: Joseph Campbell on His Life and Work*.

[2] Robert Bly (2015). *Iron John: A Book About Men*. Da Capo Press.

[3] Maureen Murdock. (2020). *The Heroine's Journey: Women's Quest for Wholeness*. Shambhala.

[4] The classic popular press book on this topic is Amir Levine and Rachel Heller's (2012) book *Attached: The New Science of Adult Attachment and How it Can Help You Find – and Keep – Love* (Tarcher Perigree). There is also a 2021 commentary in the New York Times, "Are You Anxious, Avoidant, or Secure?" (https://www.nytimes.com/2021/11/06/style/anxious-avoidant-secure-attached-book.html)

[5] Martha R. Mahoney. (1992). *Exit: Power and the Idea of Leaving in Love, Work, and the Confirmation Hearings*. (65 S. Cal. L. Rev. 1283). See also Sarah M. Buel. (1999). Fifty Obstacles to Leaving, or Why Abuse Victims Stay. *The Colorado Lawyer*. (http://sdcedsv.org/media/sdcedsvfactor360com/uploads/Articles/50Obstacles.pdf).

[6] See Jamie Ducharme's (August 1, 2018) *Time* article, "The sunk cost fallacy is ruining your decisions. Here's how."

[7] See Ryan Doody's 2020 provocative article "Sunk cost 'fallacy' is not a fallacy" in *Ergo*, 6, 40, pp. 1153-1190 (https://philarchive.org/archive/DOOTSC)

[8] There are many articles about the investment model with regards to leaving abusive relationships. See, for example, Caryl Rusbult, John Martz and Christopher Agnew's 1998 article, "The Investment Model Scale: Measuring commitment level, satisfaction level, quality of alternatives, and investment size" in *Personal Relationships*, 5, 4, 357-387 (https://doi.org/10.1111/j.1475-6811.1998.tb00177.x) and Benjamin Le and Christopher R. Agnew's review paper, "Commitment and its theorized determinants: A meta-analysis of the investment model in

Personal Relationships, *10*, 1, 37-57. (https://doi.org/10.1111/1475-6811.00035).

[9] A general overview of loss aversion is at Ulrich Schmidt & Horst Zank's (2005) article, "What is Loss Aversion?" in *Journal of Risk and Uncertainty*, *30*, 2, 157-167. (https://www.jstor.org/stable/41761190)

[10] A general overview of opportunity cost is available at Stephen Palmer and James Raftery's (1999) article "Economic Notes: opportunity cost." In *BMJ*, *318*, 7197, 1551–1552. https://doi.org/10.1136/bmj.318.7197.1551

[11] The Decision Lab has a good discussion about the status quo bias at https://thedecisionlab.com/biases/statu-quo-bias/

[12] Steven D. Levitt. (2021). Heads or tails: The impact of a coin toss on major life decisions and subsequent happiness. *Review of Economic Studies*, *88*, 378-405. (https://doi.org/10.1093/restud/rdaa016)

[13] For books about shamanism that cover these concepts, see Mircea Eliadne's (2004) *Shamanism: Archaic Techniques of Ecstasy* (Princeton University Press), Caroline Myss's (2013) *Anatomy of the Spirit: The Seven Strategies of Power and Healing* (Harmony), and Alberto Villoldo's (2000) book *Shaman, Healer, Sage: How to Heal Yourself and Others with the Energy Medicine of the Americas* (Harmony).

Chapter 2

[1] See: Ian Cook's (2021) article in *Harvard Business Review* "Who is Driving the Great Resignation?" (https://hbr.org/2021/09/who-is-driving-the-great-resignation); Derek's Thompson's (2021) article in *The Atlantic* (https://www.theatlantic.com/ideas/archive/2021/10/great-resignation-accelerating/620382/); and Arianne Cohen's (2021) article in *Bloomberg Businessweek*, "Job in the Great Post-Pandemic Resignation Boom" (https://www.bloomberg.com/news/articles/2021-05-10/quit-your-job-how-to-resign-after-covid-pandemic?sref=BGQFqz7X)

[2] According to the Bureau of Labor Statistics at https://www.bls.gov/news.release/jolts.nr0.htm

[3] See Colette Allred's (2019) "Gray divorce rate in the U.S.: Geographic variation, 2017" at https://www.bgsu.edu/content/dam/BGSU/college-of-arts-and-sciences/NCFMR/documents/FP/fp-19-20-gray-divorce-geo-var.pdf

[4] See Gallup poll reporting at https://news.gallup.com/poll/201731/lgbt-identification-rises.aspx

[5] See Daniel Cox and Robert Jones' (2017) report on "America's Changing Religious Identity" at https://www.prri.org/research/american-religious-landscape-christian-religiously-unaffiliated/ . See also Derek Thompson's (2019) article in *The Atlantic,* 'Three Decades Ago, America Lost Its Religion. Why?" at https://academyll.org/wordpress/assets/Thompson%E2%80%94Three-Decades-Ago-America-Lost-its-Religion-why.pdf

[6] See the Pew Research Center's (2015) report on "The Future of World Religions: Population Growth Projections, 2010-2050" at https://www.pewforum.org/2015/04/02/religious-projections-2010-2050/

[7] Dan Way. (2018). "Is it ever okay to quit? Five reasons not to run." *Canadian Running* https://runningmagazine.ca/sections/training/training-tips-when-to-throw-in-the-towel/

[8] Leaving high school: Joel McFarland, Jiashan Cui & Patrick Stark's "Trends in High School Dropout and Completion Rates in the United States: 2014" at https://files.eric.ed.gov/fulltext/ED581122.pdf). Leaving medical school: Lotte Dyhrberg O'Neill, Birgitta Wallstedt, Berit Eika, & Jan Hartvigsen (2011). Factors associated with dropout in medical education: a literature review. *Medical Education in Review.* (https://doi.org/10.1111/j.1365-2923.2010.03898.x); Leaving graduate school: (https://www.science.org/content/article/it-s-ok-quit-your-phd)

[9] Robin Westmacott and John Hunsley (2010). Reasons for terminating psychotherapy: A general population study. *Journal of Clinical Psychology, 66,* 9, 965-977. (https://doi.org/10.1002/jclp.20702).

[10] Jeremiah, J., O'Sullivan, P. & Stein, M.D. (1995). Who leaves against medical advice?. *Journal of General Internal Medicine, 10,* 403–405 (https://doi.org/10.1007/BF02599843)

[11] Elizabeth Mayfield Arnold. (1999). The Cessation of Cancer Treatment as a Crisis. *Social Work in Health Care, 2,* 21-38.

[12] Lana Bortolot (February 21, 2020). Taking the Expat Leap. *New York Times*, page RE1.

[13] See, for example, Stephanie Lee's (2018) *New York Times* article, "Sometimes You Have to Quit to Get Ahead." (https://www.nytimes.com/2018/06/05/smarter-living/knowing-when-to-quit.html), Tim Herrera's (2019) *New York Times* article "Giving Up Is Sometimes the Best Way to Solve a Problem

(https://www.nytimes.com/2019/05/05/smarter-living/giving-up-is-not-the-same-thing-as-failing.html), and Anisa Purbasari Horton's (2019) article in *Fast Company*, "When is it appropriate to give up on a goal?" (https://www.fastcompany.com/90297559/when-is-it-appropriate-to-give-up-on-a-goal)

14 See Richard Fry, Jeffrey S. Passel, and D'Vera Cohn's (2020) report from the Pew Research Center, "A majority of young adults in the U.S. live with their parents for the first time since the Great Depression" (https://www.pewresearch.org/fact-tank/2020/09/04/a-majority-of-young-adults-in-the-u-s-live-with-their-parents-for-the-first-time-since-the-great-depression/)

15 The angry exit was performed by JetBlue flight attendant Steven Slater at John F. Kennedy International Kennedy airport in 2010 after a disagreement with a passenger.

16 Pamela Slim (2009). *Escape from Cubicle Nation: From Corporate Prisoner to Thriving Entrepreneur*. Berkeley.

17 Amber Coverdale Sumrall (1994). *Breaking Up is Hard to Do: Stories by Women*. Crossing Press.

18 See the 1981 article by Zick Rubin, Letitia Anne Peplau, & Charles T. Hill, "Loving and Leaving: Sex Differences in Romantic Attachments" in *Sex Roles, 7*, 8, 821-835.

19 Dorothy Allison. (1994). *Skin: Talking about Sex, Class and Literature*. Firebrand Books. Pages 19-20.

20 For information on Americans' and other nationalities' moving patterns, see Adam Chandler's (2016) article in *The Atlantic*, "Why do Americans move so much more than Europeans?" (https://www.theatlantic.com/business/archive/2016/10/us-geographic-mobility/504968/) and Neli Esipova, Anita Pugliese, & Julie Ray's (2013) article from *Gallup*, "381 Million Adults Worldwide Migrate Within Countries" (https://bit.ly/3FQBkmg)

21 See Jenny Offill and Elissa Schappell (Editors) (2007) *The Friend Who Got Away: Twenty Women's True Life Tales of Friendships that Blew Up, Burned Out or Faded Away* (Broadway Books) and Jessica Smock and Stephanie Sprenger (Editors). (2014) *My Other Ex: Women's True Stories of Losing and Leaving Friends* (HerStories Project Press).

22 Martha Beck. (2006). *Leaving the Saints: How I Lost the Mormons and Found My Faith*. Broadway Books. Page 263.

[23] William Lobdell. (2009). *Losing My Religion: How I Lost My Faith Reporting on Religion in America – and Found Unexpected Peace.* Harper.

[24] Ibid.

[25] John Steinbeck. (1961/1997). *Travels with Charley in Search of America.* Penguin. Page 3.

[26] William Finnegan. (2015). *Barbarian Days: A Surfing Life.* Penguin. Page 148.

[27] Bonnie Morris's (1995) article, "A Different Bookworm: Coming Out, Brainy-Girl Style" is a delightful read. *NWSA Journal, 7,* 1, Pages 91-97.

[28] A good overview on desistance from criminal life is in Fergus McNeill, Stephen Farrall, Claire Lightowler and Shadd Maruna's (2012) article, "How and why people stop offending: Discovering desistance," available at (https://www.iriss.org.uk/resources/insights/how-why-people-stop-offending-discovering-desistance)

[29] Elizabeth Gilbert made this comment on Facebook on February 28, 2006 in response to a meme she posted that said, "When life is stressful, do something to life your spirits. Go for a drive. Go two or three thousand miles away. Maybe change your name."

Chapter 3

[1] Martha Beck. (2006). *Leaving the Saints: How I Lost the Mormons and Found My Faith.* Broadway Books. Page 327.

[2] Viktor Frankl. (2006). *Man's Search for Meaning.* Beacon Press.

Chapter 4

[1] James Hollis. (2013). *Hauntings: Dispelling the Ghosts Who Run Our Lives.* Chiron Publications.

[2] Cheryl Strayed. (2012). *Wild: From Lost to Found on the Pacific Crest Trail.* Random House. p. 57

[3] Aristotle. (2019). *Nicomachean Ethics, 3rd Edition.* Hackett Publishing Company, Inc.

[4] As suggested in Kenneth Michael Lamb's (2014) dissertation, "A Commonwealth of Hope: Virtue, Rhetoric, and Religion in Augustine's Political Thought." (http://arks.princeton.edu/ark:/88435/dsp019g54xk88w)

[5] Lucius Seneca. (2020) *Letters from a Stoic.* William Collins.

[6] René Descartes (2016). *The Passions of the Soul and Other Late Philosophical Writings* (Oxford University Press) includes his statement that hope is the soul's desire to believe a dream will come true.

[7] Friedrich Nietzsche (1883/1974). *Thus Spoke Zarathustra*. Penguin. Also, Friedrich Nietzsche 1878/1996). *Human, All Too Human*. Cambridge University Press

[8] See Charles R. Snyder's (1995) article, "Conceptualizing, measuring, and nurturing hope" in the *Journal of Counseling and Development, 73*, 3.

[9] John Steinbeck. (1961/1997) *Travels with Charley in Search of America*. Penguin. Page 5.

[10] Susan Jeffers. (1987). *Feel the Fear and Do It Anyway*. Jeffers Press and Susan Jeffers. (2007). *Embracing Uncertainty*. St. Martin's Press.

[11] Alexis Jetter interviewed Dorothy Allison in her (1995) article, "The Roseanne of Literature" in the *New York Times*. https://www.nytimes.com/1995/12/17/magazine/the-roseanne-of-literature.html

Chapter 5

[1] For a good overview on self-efficacy, see review article by Heslin, P.A., & Klehe, U.C. (2006). Self-efficacy. In S. G. Rogelberg (Ed.), *Encyclopedia of Industrial/Organizational Psychology* (Vol. 2). pp. 705-708. Thousand Oaks: Sage. (https://ssrn.com/abstract=1150858)

[2] Max Erhmann (1927). "Desiderata." As published in Bertha Pratt King Ehrmann (1948). *The Poems of Max Ehrmann*. Bruce Humphries Inc.

[3] Susan Jeffers. (1987). *Feel the Fear and Do It Anyway*. Jeffers Press.

Chapter 6

[1] Cheryl Strayed. (2012). *Wild: From Lost to Found on the Pacific Crest Trail*. Random House. Page 9.

[2] Tim Ferris. (2009). *The Four-Hour Work Week* (Harmony).

[3] This quote is attributed to a workshop Esther Hicks hosted in Orlando, Florida on February 21, 1998.

Chapter 7

[1] Marilyn Harris. (1971). *The Runaway's Diary*. Four Winds Press. Pages 209-210.

[2] Martha Beck. *(2006). Leaving the Saints: How I Lost the Mormons and Found My Faith.* Broadway Books.

[3] John Steinbeck. (1961/1997). *Travels with Charley in Search of America.* Penguin. Page 3.

[4] Author William Gibson said, "Scenarios have to be plausible, but reality is under no such constraints," in a 2011 interview with Garry Peterson in *Resilience Science* entitled, "William Gibson does not think our present was anyone's future." (https://rs.resalliance.org/2011/11/01/william-gibson-interviewed/)

Chapter 8

[1] Dorothy Allison. (1996). *Two or Three Things I Know For Sure.* Penguin Books. Page 48.

[2] Marilyn Harris. (1971). *The Runaway's Diary.* Four Winds Press. Page 6.

[3] Audre Lorde. (1982). *Zami: A New Spelling of My Name.* Persephone Press. Page 104.

[4] Turkish playwright and novelist Mehmet Murat Ildan suggests, "Leaving a place, a person or a country silently and without any notice is a heroic and a noble way of teaching the importance of your presence to those who ignore your existence."

[5] Marilyn Harris. (1971). *The Runaway's Diary.* Four Winds Press, Page 3.

[6] David Sbarra, Hillary Smith, and Matthias Mehl. (2012). When leaving your ex, love yourself: Observational ratings of self-compassion predict the course of emotional recovery following marital separation. *Psychological Science, 23,* 3, pp. 261-269. (https://www.jstor.org/stable/41441783)

Chapter 9

[1] Martha Beck. *Leaving the Saints: How I Lost the Mormons and Found My Faith* (Broadway Books, 2006). Page 322.

[2] Susan Jeffers. (1987). *Feel the Fear and Do It Anyway.* Jeffers Press.

[3] Marilyn Harris. (1971). *The Runaway's Diary.* Four Winds Press. Page 210.

[4] Martha Beck. (2006). *Leaving the Saints: How I Lost the Mormons and Found My Faith.* Broadway Books. Page 325.

Chapter 10

[1] See, for example, James Hollis. (2005) *Finding Meaning in the Second Half of Life* (Avery) and James Hollis (2009) *What Matters Most* (Avery).

[2] See, for example, Amber Coverdale Sumrall. (1994). *Breaking Up is Hard to Do: Stories by Women* (Crossing Press); Jenny Offill and Elissa Schappell (Editors) (2007) *The Friend Who Got Away: Twenty Women's True Life Tales of Friendships that Blew Up, Burned Out or Faded Away* (Broadway Books); and Jessica Smock and Stephanie Sprenger (Editors) (2014) *My Other Ex: Women's True Stories of Losing and Leaving Friends* (HerStories Project Press).

[3] For more on sense of agency, see James W. Moore's (2016) article, "What is the sense of agency and why does it matter?" in *Frontiers in Psychology*, 7, 1272 (doi: 10.3389/fpsyg.2016.01272).

[4] Viktor Frankl. (2006). *Man's Search for Meaning*. Beacon Press.

[5] Thich Nhat Hanh. (2005). *Touching Peace*. Parallax Press.

[6] Melody Beattie, author of 1986's bestseller *Codependent No More: How to Stop Controlling Others and Start Caring for Yourself* (Hazleden), said that mistakes are recyclable on her blog at https://melodybeattie.com/gods-will-day-1/

Chapter 11

[1] In David Scheff's (1981) "The John Lennon Interview" published in January 1981's *Playboy*.

Chapter 12

[1] Elizabeth Gilbert made this comment on Facebook on February 28, 2006 in response to a meme she posted that said, "When life is stressful, do something to life your spirits. Go for a drive. Go two or three thousand miles away. Maybe change your name."

[2] John Steinbeck. (1961/1997). *Travels with Charley in Search of America*. Penguin. Page 9.

[3] Susan Jeffers. (2007). *Embracing Uncertainty*. St. Martin's Press. Pages 11-12.

[4] John Watson. (1903). *The Homely Virtues*. Hodder & Stoughton. Page 168.

[5] André Gide. (1925). *Les faux-monnayeurs* [The Counterfeiters]. Vintage International.

[6] Dorothy Allison. (2002). *Trash: Stories*. Penguin Books. Page 6.

Acknowledgements

This book has truly been a labor of love. I am grateful to those who supported and encouraged me throughout this process, including Lourdes, Linda, Billy, Katrina, Tara, Amy, Diego, Jeff, Ramani, Sarah, the Wonk crew, Jeremy, Phil, Leah, Sunny, and many others. I appreciate my mother's consultation and feedback as we reconciled our leaving and staying experiences.

Special thanks to Cassandra Blake, Lindsay Harris, Shannon Golden, and Gerry Vogel for valuable research support. Thank you to Martha Bullen for publishing consultation.

Finally, I especially appreciate all of those who told me their heartfelt leaving stories and allowed me the honor to witness their struggles, challenges, growth, and success. I hope we all have the courage to leave what is no longer working.

About the Author

Jennifer P. Wisdom, PhD, is a licensed clinical psychologist, author, consultant, adventurer, and leaver. She has a doctorate in clinical psychology, a Master of Public Health in Biostatistics and Epidemiology, and national board certification in organizational and business consulting psychology. Her diverse experience includes serving in the U.S. military, consulting to nonprofit health care organizations, teaching in higher education, and being a TEDx speaker.

She is the author of the best-selling *Millennials' Guides* series, including *Millennials' Guide to Management and Leadership*, *Millennials' Guide to Relationships*, and *Millennials' Guide to Work*. She hosts the podcast *Millennial Wisdom*.

She has left jobs in retail, journalism, the military, newspaper and academic journal editing, therapy, academia, and education. She has left home, left the country, left a spouse, left partners, ended friendships, and left for adventure. She has lived in more than 27 places she called home.

She runs her own consulting firm, Wisdom Consulting (www.leadwithwisdom.com), and publishing company (www.windingpathwaybooks.com). She is also affiliated faculty at Oregon Health and Science University, and Portland State University. She currently splits her time between New York City and Portland, Oregon.

Made in USA - North Chelmsford, MA
1299258_9781954374423
01.19.2022 0939

Made in USA - North Chelmsford, MA
1299258_9781954374423
01.19.2022 0939